# Entrepreneur.

# WRITE YOUR BUSINESS PLAN

## YOUR STEP-BY-STEP GUIDE TO BUILDING A THRIVING BUSINESS

## SECOND EDITION

### BY THE STAFF OF ENT~~REPRENEUR~~ AND ERIC ~~BUTOW~~

Entrepreneur

Entrepreneur Press, Publisher
Cover Design: Andrew Welyczko
Production and Composition: Faith & Family Publications

This publication is designed to provide accurate and authoritative information in regard
to the subject matter covered. It is sold with the understanding that the publisher is not
engaged in rendering legal, accounting, or other professional services. If legal advice
or other expert assistance is required, the services of a competent professional person
should be sought.

**Library of Congress Cataloging-in-Publication Data**
Names: Butow, Eric, author. | Entrepreneur Press, author. Title: Write your your
     business plan : a step-by-step guide to build your business / by The Staff of
     Entrepreneur Media and Eric Butow.
Description: 2nd Edition. | Irvine : Entrepreneur Press, [2023] | Revised edition.
     | Summary: "Write Your Business Plan, 2nd Edition is the essential guide that
     leads you through the most critical startup step next to committing to your
     business vision-writing your business plan"—Provided by publisher.
Identifiers: LCCN 2023015592 (print) | LCCN 2023015593 (ebook) | ISBN
     9781642011586 (paperback) | ISBN 9781613084694 (epub)
Subjects: LCSH: Business planning. | New business enterprises—Management.
     | Small business—Management. Classification: LCC HD30.28 .B8688 2023
     (print) | LCC HD30.28 (ebook) | DDC 658.4/012—dc23/ eng/20230421
LC record available at https://lccn.loc.gov/2023015592
LC ebook record available at https://lccn.loc.gov/2023015593

26  25  24  23                                          10 9 8 7 6 5 4 3 2 1

# Contents

# Foreword by Jesse Draper

I owe a lot of my success to that guy in the Transporter movies, and he has no idea.

Let me take you back to a simpler time. I was living in Santa Monica with three friends from UCLA and a cavalier King Charles named Archie. I was also spending most of my time filming the second season of a Nickelodeon show where I played a babysitter conveniently named Jesse. And I was auditioning a lot.

I know. This is not where most stories about venture capital and entrepreneurship start. But stick with me here. I started my career in acting.

Anyway, I went to a casting call and "Transporter Dude" was sitting in the corner in a long black trench coat alongside a few casting directors. It was an audition for *Transporter 2* or maybe *3*? Are there three? They don't ask my name. They don't make small talk. This is an efficient, if dehumanizing, machine. They take my picture. "Turn around." *Snap.* "Turn around." *Snap.* And Transporter Dude is just sitting there. In that moment I felt so . . . deeply uncomfortable. I felt disgusting and I knew I needed a change, but I was a twenty-something actress; what choice did I have during a time when Paris Hilton and Lindsay Lohan were scantily clad on the cover of magazines? Serendipitously, I was invited to the first Twitter conference at the Skirball Cultural Center in LA because I was some kind of Z-list Nickelodeon celebrity. I looked around. Men in suits and hoodies. A few ladies (not many). Having grown up around entrepreneurs and innovation in Silicon Valley (before it was a TV show), I felt oddly more comfortable there. I felt some passion reignite in me talking about the future of "microblogging" with other people who loved technology.

If you're picking up this book, you can probably relate. I think we all have that moment where, although it might seem insignificant at the time, it's the turning point of your life. The moment you decide you are not going to accept anything less than going after that path or business idea that's been brewing in the back of your mind.

So, I went back to work on Nickelodeon's *The Naked Brothers Band* (that was the show), and asked our producers if I could sit in on production meetings. I had an idea for my own show, but I had no idea where to start. I gathered up enough knowledge that I felt comfortable starting my own production company. There, I launched *The Valley Girl Show*, a quirky, lighthearted talk show where I featured the best and brightest minds of Silicon Valley. This was a way into that technology world I wanted so badly to be part of—it was the best of both worlds.

It was also a way to take control—of my time, my income, and my future. After two seasons, I brought on a business partner, Jonathan Polenz, and we started building out a technology news site, ValleyLoop, and then acquired the only LA technology news site of the time, Lalawag. We were one of the first video content companies to partner with Forbes.com and Mashable with technology content that was digestible and maybe too silly.

After two seasons of the show and millions of passive eye balls in Denny's restaurants and on gas station screens, I'd talked to a lot of incredible men who were building technology companies—I was one of the first people to ever interview Drew Houston, which ended up on the cover of the *New York Times* Style Section in an article about my show by an incredible journalist named Laura Houston; I interviewed former Google CEO Eric Schmidt; and I sat down with Elon Musk (before the drama), and while it's probably my most googleable interview, I'm pretty sure both Elon and I wish it would disappear due to my ditzy and pink persona. Think Ali G. of technology and maybe too real? I digress again. After this ditziness overload with men in tech, I made an initiative to interview 50 percent women in tech and shifted the show a bit. I started a series on the show called "Rockin' Women" and spoke to Sheryl Sandberg, Julia Hartz, Jessica Mah, Jenn Hyman, Rebecca Minkoff, and Alexis Maybank, to name a few. I started getting pitched by hundreds of businesses that were started by incredible women, and that's when the magic began. I saw the massive opportunity to invest in women. We were nominated for an Emmy and things started to happen. I had grown up as the oldest of four as well as a fourth-generation venture capitalist who constantly felt like a fraud because I was a female. I wanted to help these women in technology and shift the narrative from ditziness to IPO. I realized I could help them in two ways. First with media exposure and then with funding.

In 2015, I raised my first fund and started Halogen Ventures, an early stage technology company focused on investing in female-founded consumer technology companies. A lot of my initial investors were guests from my show. Since then, I've raised multiple funds, seen tens of thousands of pitches, funded over seventy companies (The Skimm, Babylist, ThirdLove, HopSkipDrive, The Flex Company to name a few), have had 10 exits (including Squad [acquired by Twitter], ELOQUII [sold to Walmart], and This is L [sold to P&G]), and sit on numerous boards. I've seen the good, the bad, and the ugly in founders and funders.

While there are so many factors that go into creating a successful business, building your business doesn't have to be so hard! Take the time to write a plan. This step is often underestimated or skipped. Whether you're starting a business for the first time, or revisiting your current plan, building a scalable business starts with creating a strong foundation.

I know it can be overwhelming. Now let me take you back to me on my Nickelodeon show wearing my J Brand jeans and going-out shirts, about to jump into my first entrepreneurial endeavor and starting my own business. I would spend endless hours perusing the business aisle in Barnes & Noble. There was nothing for starting a business. I wish I had this book. There were a few financial books, some Warren Buffett books, but nothing truly entrepreneurial. I also had no idea where to start. I quickly realized the power of putting pen to paper. I could have only dreamed of having a step-by-step guidebook to follow like this book. It would have been a game changer and saved a lot of time and tears.

Before you dig in, here are my three pieces of advice on starting your company.

1.  Just press go! It will never be perfect. I cannot tell you how often founders say, "Let me get my ducks in a row." Here is a little secret: Your ducks will never be in a row, and if you are a great founder, like the ones in my portfolio, you are always making it better . . . your ducks are always being iterated upon and forming more of a line. So just start!

2.  Diversity breeds success. If you look around and realize that your entire team is made up of Stanford graduates who all look the same and are the same personality type on the Myers-Briggs assessment . . . recruit from new places. At Halogen we think about diversity of age, race, and gender in our teams. When I raised my first fund, people thought I was crazy investing in women. "Do women even start companies?" Now there is so much great research on how diverse teams perform better.

3.  Get through the "Noes." While fundraising for your business, plan on meeting with at least 100 investors. I can't tell you how often entrepreneurs say, "Everyone is saying 'No.'" When I ask how many investors they have met with, they say, "Eight." First of all, this is a numbers game. After twenty or so meetings, it is great to check in and see why funders are turning down your deal and get some feedback because maybe there is something you are missing that you can adjust. But overall, plan on meeting with at least 100 investors.

Enjoy this thoughtful book on starting and growing your business. The greatest thing about entrepreneurship is that anyone with any background and any wild and crazy idea can start a company. You got this! You are meant to do this! Get out there and START! And come pitch me at Halogen Ventures. Also . . . don't credit some Transporter Dude with your own success. Use this book and you will be solely responsible for it!

Lots of Love,
Jesse Draper
Founding Partner of Halogen Ventures

# Introduction

As you start to read this book, you may be starting your own business or already have a business, but in each case you either don't have a business plan or have such an old one that it needs to be revised. And you may be overwhelmed by all the conflicting advice you find online and maybe in other books. You don't need a business plan. You need a business plan, but it can be just one page no matter if it's a printed page or handwritten on a cocktail napkin. You need a tome for a business plan that will last you for the life of your business.

But one size does not fit all businesses, because every business is different. What's more, you may need more than one business plan to approach different audiences, such as one for your employees to refer to and one for venture capitalists as they consider financing your business. No matter what business you have, you need to have a business plan to act as your company's North Star—and, let's not forget, get funding from banks and/or investors.

This book helps you determine what type of plan (or plans) you need and how to put one together. And we also tell you how to find resources that will help your new business get off the ground and keep your business thriving.

We start by telling you how to build a strong foundation for your business in Section I. This section covers the basics of what you need for your business plan, and it will get you in the right frame of mind before you move to the following two sections. Section I takes you through the fundamental questions that a business plan needs to answer. Chapter 5, which is the last chapter in Section I, also tells you how to put your business plan to work and the importance of updating your plan to respond to changing business conditions.

Section II talks about the presentation of your business in the plan. You start with an executive summary. Once you summarize your plan, you need to go into greater detail about who's helping you manage the business and what you sell. Then you can show readers the money not only with financial information, but also with revenue opportunities in your industry, how your marketing will drive revenue, and how your operations will keep up with customer demand.

Section III talks about getting your cover letter ready to present to readers when you deliver your business plan to them. If you still need more support once your business plan is done, we have you covered. Chapter 14 is chock-full of connections to associations, books, websites, and even business plan competitions. Appendix A has a long list of resources for you to check out, too.

Ready to get started? Turn to the next page to understand what you'll learn in Section I.

> Remember to redeem your complimentary 30-day access to LivePlan, a business planning and management software trusted by over 1 million small businesses, that will help you get your business off the ground. Flip to page [insert page #] to claim your offer.

# SECTION 1

# Your Foundation
# Comes First

## *Section Summary*

**W**riting a business plan is like the architectural plan for a home or a brick-and-mortar building. You need to know what materials you need, how you're going to construct the building, and when you need to build each piece of the building. You start by building the foundation, because without it your business can't stand up.

This section starts by covering the basics and asking you fundamental questions in Chapter 1. Next, Chapter 2 talks about how you need to develop a plan that's the right fit for your business—and how the right fit could mean you need more than one plan. In Chapter 3, we talk about answering the basic questions that your plan readers will want to know. One of those questions is about financing, and Chapter 4 goes into greater detail about direct and indirect funding sources. Finally, Chapter 5 talks about how to put your plan to work in your business.

## Chapter 1 Summary

A business plan is a written description of the future of your business. It is a document that tells the story of what you plan to do and how you plan to do it. If you jot down a paragraph on the back of an envelope describing your business strategy, you've written a plan, or at least the germ of a plan.

Business plans are inherently strategic. You start here, today, with certain resources and abilities. You want to get to a "there," a point in the future (usually three to five years out) at which time your business will have a different set of resources and abilities as well as greater profitability and more assets. Your plan shows how you will get from here to there. In essence it is a road map from where you are now to where you want to be later on.

What you'll learn from this chapter:

- What should be in your plan, including your concept, strategy, and your products and/or services
- The plan that's right for your business and presents you in the best light
- What your goals and objectives are
- The software you need to create your plan
- The direct and indirect funding sources for your business
- How to manage your plan as you put it to work

# Building Brick by Brick

If you've done any research about business plans online or through an agency like the Small Business Administration (SBA), you've probably heard about some generally accepted conventions about what a business plan should include and how it should be presented. In sum, a plan should cover all the important matters that will contribute to making your business a success, including:

1. *Your basic business concept.* This is where you discuss the industry, your business structure, your particular product or service, and how you plan to make your business a success. To use the analogy of building

a brick-and-mortar building, this is the concrete you use for your foundation.

2. *Your strategy and the specific actions you plan to take to implement it.* What goals do you have for your business? When and how will you reach your goals? After all, you need to know how you plan to construct your building.

3. *Your products and services and their competitive advantages.* Here is your chance to dazzle the readers with good, solid information about your products or services and why customers will want to purchase your products and services and not those of your competitors. Your products and services are the materials you'll use for the building.

4. *The markets you'll pursue. Now you have to lay out your marketing plan.* Who will your customers be? What is your demographic audience? How will you attract and retain enough customers to make a profit? What methods will you use to capture your audience? What sets your business apart from the competition? How are you going to get people to come to your building and spend money?

5. *The background of your management team and key employees.* Having information about key personnel is an important but often misrepresented portion of a business plan. It's not a long and detailed biography of each person involved but an accurate account of what they have done and what they bring to the table for this specific business opportunity. Readers will want to know who's going to construct your building and if they're qualified builders.

6. *Your financing needs.* These will be based on your projected financial statements. These statements provide a model of how your ideas about the company, its markets, and its strategies will play out. With a building, you need to know the costs of your materials as well as how you will adapt to changing conditions including pricing and construction delays due to weather.

As you write your business plan, stick to facts instead of feelings, projections instead of hopes, and realistic expectations of profit instead of unrealistic dreams of wealth. You want to show readers that your building will last for years to come. And facts—checkable, demonstrable facts—will invest your plan with the most important component of all: credibility.

## How Long Should Your Plan Be?

A useful business plan can be any length, from a one-page summary to more than 100 pages for an especially detailed plan describing a complex enterprise. A typical business plan runs fifteen to twenty-five pages, created and (usually) sent electronically, sometimes accompanied by forms the receiver requests that you fill out. Occasionally, you may still be asked for a hard copy of your plan.

Miniplans of five to ten pages are the popular concise models that may stand on their own for smaller businesses. Larger businesses, seeking major funding, will often have miniplans as well, but the full business plan will be waiting in the wings. It's to your advantage to run long when creating your plan and then narrow it down for presentation purposes.

The size of the plan will also depend on the nature of your business and your reason for writing the plan. If you have a simple concept, you may be able to express it in very few words. On the other hand, if you are proposing a new kind of business or even a new industry, it may require quite a bit of explanation to get the message across. If you are writing a plan for a division of a large organization, you may be given a set format and prescribed length.

The purpose of your plan also determines its length. If you are looking for millions of dollars in seed capital to start a risky venture, you will usually (although not always) have to do a lot of explaining and convincing. If you already have relationships with potential investors, they may simply want a miniplan. If you are just going to use your plan for internal purposes to manage an ongoing business, a much more abbreviated version may suffice. Chapter 2 goes into more detail about the structure and type of business plan you need.

If you are wanting to start small with an effective way to get your ideas down, you can follow the guidance of LivePlan, a business planning and management software, on writing your one-page plan for your business:

"Understanding the fundamentals of your business model is the first step to create a winning business plan. That's why we recommend that you start with a simple business plan that fits on a single page. LivePlan will help you clearly explain who your customers are, what your marketing and sales activities will be, and what your product or service offerings will be. It's the quickest way to get started.

"When you're starting out, having a one-page plan will help make your business memorable. LivePlan lets you share a link to your one-page plan - or export to PowerPoint - so you can quickly show your business plan to people," LivePlan, https://www.liveplan.com/features/build-your-business-pitch.

Many business plan presentations are made with PowerPoint decks, using ten to twelve slides to tell your story. This is a great starting point, but you should have at least a miniplan available, especially if you are seeking millions of dollars. More on PowerPoint presentations later.

---

### ⫸ buzzword

Competitive advantage is what makes you different from, and better than, your competition. Lower price, higher quality, and better name recognition are examples of competitive advantages. By studying your competition, you can devise your own competitive advantage by providing something (or several things) that it does not offer.

---

### Cocktail Napkin Business Plan

Business plans don't have to be complicated, lengthy documents. They just have to capture the essence of what the business will do and why it will be a success.

The business plan for one of the most successful startups ever began with a triangle scrawled on a cocktail napkin. The year was 1971, and Herb Kelleher and Rollin King were formulating their idea for an airline serving Houston, Dallas, and San Antonio. The triangle connecting the cities was their route map—and the basis of the business plan for Southwest Airlines.

The two entrepreneurs soon expressed their vision for Southwest Airlines more fully in a full-fledged business plan and raised millions in initial capital to get off the ground. Eventually they went public. Along the way, the airline expanded beyond the three cities to include other Texas destinations, and now it serves over 100 destinations in 42 states plus Washington, DC, and Puerto Rico with over 4,000 flights daily and revenues of $15.8 billion in 2021. Southwest specializes in low-cost, no-frills, high-frequency service, which, if you just add some lines to the original triangle, is the same strategy mapped out on that cocktail napkin.

## When Should You Write It?

The fact that you're reading this book means you suspect it's about time to write a business plan. Odds are you are at or near one of the many occasions when a business plan will prove useful.

- A business plan is a good way to explore the feasibility of a new business without actually having to start it and run it. A good plan can help you see serious flaws in your business concept. You may uncover tough competition when researching the market section, or you may find that your financial projections simply aren't realistic.
- Any venture that faces major changes (and that means almost all businesses) needs a business plan. If the demographics of your market are rapidly changing, strong new competitive products challenge your profitability, you expect your business to grow or shrink dramatically, or the economic climate is improving or slipping rapidly, you'll need a business plan. This will allow you to make changes accordingly.
- If you are contemplating buying or selling a business, your business plan can provide you with a handy tool to establish a value—and to support that value if challenged.
- You will need a business plan if you are seeking financing. Your business plan is the backbone of your financing proposal. Bankers, venture capitalists, and other financiers rarely provide money without seeing a plan. Less sophisticated investors or friends and family may not require a business plan, but they deserve one. Even if you're funding the business with your own savings, you owe it to yourself to plan how you'll expend the resources you're committing.

Writing a business plan is not a onetime exercise. Just because you wrote a plan when you were starting out or raising money to get underway doesn't mean you are finished. Many companies look for additional rounds of funding. By updating business plans to let investors know how the funding has been used to date, and the results of such efforts, the chances of procuring such funding are improved. A business plan should be rewritten or revised regularly to get maximum benefit from it. Commonly, business plans are revised yearly, more frequently if conditions have changed enough to make the previous plan unrealistic.

## Who Needs a Business Plan?

About the only person who doesn't need a business plan is one who's not going into business. You don't need a plan to start a hobby or to moonlight from your regular job. But anybody beginning or extending a venture that will consume significant resources of money, energy, or time and that is expected to return a profit should take the time to draft some kind of plan.

### Startups

The classic business plan writer is an entrepreneur seeking funds to help start a new venture. Many great companies had their starts in the form of a plan that was used to convince investors to put up the capital necessary to get them underway.

However, it's a mistake to think that only startups need business plans. Companies and managers find plans useful at all stages of their existence, whether they're seeking financing or trying to figure out how to invest a surplus.

### Established Firms Seeking Help

Many business plans are written by and for companies that are long past the startup stage but also well short of large-corporation status. These middle-stage enterprises may draft plans to help them find funding for growth just as the startups do, although the amounts they seek may be larger and the investors more willing because the company already has a track record. They may feel the need for a written plan to help manage an already rapidly growing business. A business plan may be seen as a valuable tool to convey the mission and prospects of the business to customers, suppliers, or other interested parties.

Just as the initial plan maps how to get from one leg of the journey to the next, an updated plan for additional funding adds another leg of your journey. It's not unlike traveling from the United States to Paris and then deciding to visit London or Barcelona or both along the way. You would then need to add to, or update, your plans. A business plan can, therefore, address the next stage in the life process of a business.

---

### 》 plan pointer

Check with your local Small Business Development Center (www. sba.gov) if you need help developing your business plan. Many colleges and universities also have small business experts available to lend a hand.

---

## 12 Reasons Why You Need a Business Plan

Business plans could be considered cheap insurance. Just as many people don't buy fire insurance on their homes and rely on good fortune to protect their investment, many successful business owners do not rely on written business plans but trust their own instincts. However, your business plan is more than insurance. It reflects your ideas, intuitions, instincts, and insights about your business and its future—and provides the cheap insurance of testing them out before you are committed to a course of action.

Beyond what we've already talked about in this chapter, there are a dozen more reasons for creating a business plan, and chances are that more than one of these reasons apply to your business.

1. **A plan helps you set specific objectives for managers**. Good management requires setting specific objectives and then tracking and following up. As your business grows, you want to organize, plan, and communicate your business priorities better to your team and to

you. Writing a plan gets everything clear in your head before you talk about it with your team.

2. **You can share your strategy, priorities, and plans with your spouse or partner.** People in your personal life intersect with your business life, so shouldn't they know what's supposed to be happening?

3. **Use the plan to explain your displacement.** A short definition of displacement is, "Whatever you do is something else you don't do." Your plan will explain why you're doing what you've decided to do in your business.

4. **A plan helps you figure out whether or not to rent or buy new space.** Do your growth prospects and plans justify taking on an increased fixed cost of new space?

5. **You can explain your strategy for hiring new people.** How will new people help your business grow and prosper? What exactly are they going to do?

6. **A plan helps you decide whether or not to bring on new assets.** How many new assets do you need, and will you buy or lease them? Use your business plan to help decide what's going to happen in the long term and how long important purchases, such as computer equipment, will last in your plan.

7. **Share your plan with your team.** Explain the business objectives in your plan with your leadership team, employees, and new hires. What's more, make selected portions of your plan part of your new employee training.

8. **Share parts of your plan with new allies to bring them aboard.** Use your plan to set targets for new alliances with complementary businesses and also disclose selected portions of your plan with those businesses as you negotiate an alliance.

9. **Use your plan when you deal with professionals.** Share selected parts of your plan with your attorneys and accountants, as well as consultants if necessary.

10. **Have all the information in your plan when you're ready to sell.** Sell your business when it's time to put it on the market so you can help buyers understand what you have, what it's worth, and why they want it.

11. **A plan helps you set the valuation of the business.** Valuation means how much your business is worth, and it applies to formal transactions related to divorce, inheritance, estate planning, and tax issues. Usually that takes a business plan as well as a professional with experience. The plan tells the valuation expert what your business is doing, when it's doing (or will do) certain things, why those things are being done, how much that work will cost, and the benefits that work will produce.

12. **You can use information in the plan when you need cash.** Seek investment for a business no matter what stage of growth the business finds itself in. Investors need to see a business plan before they decide whether or not to invest. They'll expect the plan to cover all the main points.

"Imagine you're setting out on a journey. You know what your final destination is, but you haven't figured out how to get there. While it might be fun to just start driving and figure things out as you go, your trip will most likely take longer than you anticipated and cost you more. If you instead take a look at a map and chart the best way to get to your destination, you'll arrive on time and on budget. Planning for your business isn't that much different.

The primary purpose of a business plan is to help you figure out where you want to go with your business and how you're going to get there. It helps you set your direction and determine a winning strategy. A solid business plan will set your business up for success and help you build an unbeatable company."

Noah Parsons, "15 Reasons Why You Need a Business Plan", LivePlan, https://www.liveplan.com/blog/reasons-why-you-need-a-business-plan/, 1/1/22

## Benefits for You

If you and/or someone on your team are still skeptical about the benefits of a business plan and how it will benefit you personally, consider some advantages that can help in your day-to-day management:

- ▷ *Your educated guesses will be better.* Use your plan to refine your educated guesses about things like potential markets, sales drivers, lead processing, and business processes.
- ▷ *Priorities will make more sense.* Aside from the strategy, there are also priorities for other factors of your business including growth, management, and financial health. Use your plan to set a foundation for these, then you can revise them as the business evolves.
- ▷ *You'll understand interdependencies.* Use a plan to keep track of what needs to happen and in what order. For example, if you have to time a product release to dovetail with your marketing efforts, your business plan can be invaluable in keeping you organized and on track.
- ▷ *You'll be better at delegating.* The business plan must make clear who is responsible for what. Every important task should have one person in charge.
- ▷ *Managing team members and tracking results will be easy.* The plan is a great format for putting responsibilities and expectations in writing. Then during team member reviews, you can look to your plan to spot the differences between expectations and results so that you can make course corrections.
- ▷ *You can better plan and manage cash flow.* A cash flow plan within your overall business plan helps you and your leadership team make better educated guesses about sales, costs, expenses, assets you need to buy, and debts you have to pay.

## What Are Your Objectives?

You need to think of what you want and whether your plan's findings suggest you'll get it. For instance, is your objective to gain freedom from control by other people? If your plan shows that you'll have to take on several equity partners, each of whom will desire a chunk of ownership, you may need to come up with a business that does not require capital needs that are very intensive.

Perhaps you want a company that will let you do your work and get home at a reasonable hour, even a business you can start from home. There are so many options when it comes to starting a business, including the size, location, and, of course, the reason for existence. You will be able to determine all of these and so many more aspects of business with the help of your business plan. It forces you to think through all of the areas that form the main concept to the smallest details. This way you don't find yourself remembering at the last minute that your website is still not developed or that you still have most of your inventory in a warehouse and no way to ship it.

## Predict the Future

It may seem dishonest to say that a business plan can't predict the future. What are all those projections and forecasts for if they are not attempts to predict the future? The fact is, no projection or forecast is really a hard-and-fast prediction of the future. Not even the French seer Nostradamus could tell you for sure how your business will be doing in five years. The best you can do is have a plan in which you logically and systematically attempt to show what will happen if a particular scenario occurs. That scenario has been determined by your research and analysis to be the most likely one of the many that may occur. But it's still just a probability, not a guarantee.

You can, however, use your research, sales forecasts, market trends, and competitive analysis to make well-thought-out predictions of how you see your business developing if you are able to follow a specified course. To some extent, you can create your future rather than simply trying to predict it by the decisions you make. For example, you may not have a multimillion-dollar business in ten years if you are trying to start and run a small family business. Your decision on growth would therefore factor into your predictions and the outcome.

### Guarantee Funding

There are all kinds of reasons why a venture capitalist, banker, or other investor may refuse to fund your company. It may be that there's no money to give out at the moment. It may be that the investor just backed a company very similar to your own and now wants something different. Perhaps the investor has just promised to back her brother-in-law's firm or is merely having a bad day and saying no to everything that crosses her desk. The point is that the quality of your plan may have little or nothing to do with your prospects for getting funded by a particular investor.

But what about the investment community as a whole? Surely if you show a well-prepared plan to a lot of people, someone will be willing to back you, right? Again, not necessarily. Communities, as well as people, are subject to fads, and your idea may be yesterday's fad. Conversely, it may be too far ahead of its time. It also may be an idea that comes about in a shaky economy or a saturated market. Timing is sometimes a factor that is out of your control.

The same is true of the availability of funds. At times, banks everywhere seem to clamp down on lending, refusing to back even clearly superior borrowers. In many countries, there is no network of venture capitalists to back fledgling companies.

**Focus on Value**

For the early-stage company, the business plan is often viewed solely as a key part of obtaining financing. A business plan that effectively helps the company obtain financing will clearly communicate the company's value, the customer problems solved by the company's product, and the important investments required to bring those products to market. Maintaining your focus on these items is critical to the growth of a strong company, so a plan that clearly articulates these items should also be used in the management of the growing company.

Companies that plan grow 30 percent faster than those that don't plan... [while] plenty of businesses can find success without planning, but businesses with a plan grow faster and are more successful than those that don't plan.

Noah Parsons, "Do You Need a Business Plan? Scientific Research Says Yes", Bplans, https://www.bplans.com/business-planning/basics/research/, 3/8/23

### *Raise All the Money You'll Need*

A business plan cannot guarantee that you will raise all the money you need at any given time, especially during the startup phase. Even if you are successful in finding an investor, odds are good that you won't get quite what you asked for. There may be a big difference in what you have to give up, such as majority ownership or control, to get the funds. Or you may be able to make minor adjustments if you cannot snare as large a chunk of cash as you want.

In a sense, a business plan used for seeking funding is part of a negotiation taking place between you and your prospective financial backers. The part of the plan where you describe your financial needs can be considered your opening bid in this negotiation. The other information it contains, from market research to management bios, can be considered supporting arguments. If you look at it in that way, a business plan is an excellent opening bid. It's definite, comprehensive, and clear.

But it's still just a bid, and you know what happens to bids in negotiations. They get whittled away, the terms get changed, and, sometimes, the whole negotiation breaks down under the force of an ultimatum from one of the parties involved. Does this mean you should ask for a good deal more money than you actually need in your plan? Actually, that may not be the best strategy either. Investors who see a lot of plans are going to notice if you're asking for way too much money. Such a move stands a good chance of alienating those who might otherwise be enthusiastic backers of your plan. It's probably a better idea to ask for a little more than you think you can live with, plus slightly better terms than you really expect.

### *Fool People*

A professional financier such as a bank loan officer or a venture capitalist will see literally hundreds of business plans in the course of a year. After this has gone on for several years, and the financier has backed some percentage of those plans and seen how events have turned out, he or she becomes very good at weeding out plans with inconsistencies or overblown projections and zeroing in on weaknesses, including some you'd probably rather not see highlighted.

If you've seen the television show *Shark Tank,* you'll understand how shrewd those individuals with the dollars can be. In short, most financiers are expert plan analyzers. You have little chance of fooling one of them with an overly optimistic or even downright dishonest plan. That doesn't mean you shouldn't make the best case you honestly can for your business. But the key word is "honestly."

You certainly shouldn't play down your strengths in a plan, but don't try to hide your weaknesses either. Intelligent, experienced financiers will see them anyway. Let's say you propose to open a small health food store at an address a block away from a Whole Foods. An investor who knows this fact but doesn't see any mention of it in your plan may suspect you've lost your senses—and who could blame her?

Now think about the effect if your plan notes the existence of that big grocery store. That gives you a chance to differentiate yourself explicitly, pointing out that you'll be dealing only in locally produced foods—which the superstore doesn't carry but many of its customers may want. Suddenly that high-volume operator becomes a helpful traffic builder, not a dangerous competitor.

So, recognize and deal appropriately with the weaknesses in your plan rather than sweeping them under the rug. If you do it right, this troubleshooting can become one of the strongest parts of the whole plan.

## Business Planning Risks

There are risks associated with writing a business plan. That's right: While one of the main purposes of a business plan is to help you avoid risk, the act of creating one does create a few risks as well. These risks include:

» *The possible disclosure of confidential material.* Although most of the people who see your plan will respect its confidentiality, a few may (either deliberately or by mistake) disclose proprietary information. For this reason, you may want to have a nondisclosure agreement, or NDA, signed before sending it to others.

» *Leading yourself astray.* You may come to believe too strongly in the many forecasts and projects in your business plan.

» *Ruining your reputation . . . or worse.* If you purposely fill the plan with overly optimistic prognostication, exaggeration, or even falsehoods, you will do yourself a disservice. Some plans prepared for the purpose of seeking funds may run afoul of securities laws if they appear to be serving as prospectuses unblessed by the regulators.

» *Spending too much effort planning.* You then may not have enough energy or time to actually run your business. Some call it "analysis paralysis." It's a syndrome that occurs when you spend so much time planning that you never do anything. For a lot of businesspeople, this is a nonissue—they detest planning so much that there's no chance at all they'd forgo actually doing business and merely plan it.

Business planning can take on a life of its own. It's possible to spend so much time planning a startup that you miss your window of opportunity or to schedule such frequent updates of a plan for an established business that it becomes difficult to administer its other details. Big corporations have large staffs, which can be devoted to year-round planning. As a small business owner, you have to be more selective.

Your planning may be approaching the paralysis stage if you find yourself soothing your nerves about starting a business by delaying the startup date so you can plan more. If you notice yourself putting off crucial meetings so you can dig up more information for a plan update, suspect that planning has become overly important.

» *Diluting the effectiveness of your plan.* If you put too much detail into your plan, you run the risk of overburdening anybody who reads it with irrelevant, obscuring detail. A plan isn't supposed to be a potboiler, but it should tell a story—the story of your business.

Therefore, it should be as easy as possible to read. That means keeping technical jargon under control and making it readable in one sitting.

Explain any terms that may be unfamiliar to a reader who's not an expert on your industry. And never make the mistake of trying to overawe a reader with your expertise. There's a good chance someone reading your plan will know more than you do. If you come across as an overblown pretender, you can bet your plan will get short shrift.

It's easy to believe that a longer, more detailed plan is always better than a short, concise one. But financiers and others to whom you may send your plan are busy people. They do not have time to plow through an inches-thick plan and may in fact be put off by its imposing appearance. Better to keep it to a couple dozen pages and stick to the truly important material.

▷ *Expediting your plan.* While some insist on endless planning, others try to speed up the process. In an effort to get a plan written quickly to show a potential investor, you may find yourself cutting corners or leaving out vital information. You don't want to take forever to prepare a business plan but using some of the business plan software programs can make it so easy that you find yourself letting the programs do more of the work. Remember, the tools are there to guide you and not the other way around. Give yourself enough time to make sure that

- each section says what you want it to say
- all of your numbers add up and make sense
- you have answers to anything readers could possibly ask you

**Adding Icing to the Cake . . . or Plan**

They say rules are made to be broken. While you don't want to go out of your way to go against the grain, sometimes that is just what needs to be done. For example, a business plan for a chain of coffee shops can include photos of the proposed location, mock-ups of menus, and maps of the competition's locations. The graphics make the plan longer, but they added real value. Product shots, location shots, blueprints, floor plans, logos, and screenshots of your website can be useful for any type of retail business even if they make the plan a little longer than the norm.

## What Not to Include in a Business Plan

- *Form over substance.* If it looks good but doesn't have a solid basis in fact and research, you might as well save your energy.
- *Empty claims.* If you make a statement without supporting it, you may as well leave it out. You need to follow up what you say in the next sentence with a statistic, fact, or even a quote from a knowledgeable source that supports the claim.
- *Rumors about the competition.* If you know for sure a competitor is going out of business, you can allude to it but avoid listing its weaknesses or hearsay. Stick to facts.
- *Superlatives and strong adjectives.* Words like "major," "incredible," "amazing," "outstanding," "unbelievable," "terrific," "great," "most," "best," and "fabulous" don't have a place in a business plan. Avoid "unique" unless you can demonstrate with facts that the product or service is truly one of a kind. (Hint: Chances are, it isn't.) The same goes for hyperbole. Let the positives of your business speak for themselves.
- *Long documents.* If they want more, they will ask.
- *Overestimating on your financial projections.* Sure, you want to look good, but resist optimism here. Use half of what you think is reasonable. Better to underestimate than set expectations that aren't fulfilled.
- *Overly optimistic time frames.* Ask around or do research on the internet. If it takes most companies six to twelve months to get up and running, that is what it will take yours. If you think it will take three months to develop your prototype, double it. You will

face delays you don't know about yet—ones you can't control. Remember to be conservative in your time predictions.

▷ *Gimmicks.* Serious investors want facts, not gimmicks. They may eat the chocolate rose that accompanies the business plan for your new florist shop, but it won't make them any more interested in investing in the venture.

▷ *Amateurish financial projections.* Spend some money and get an accountant to do these for you. They'll help you think through the financial side of your venture, plus put the numbers into a standard business format that a businessperson expects.

---

"The absolute biggest business plan mistake you can make is to not plan at all. That doesn't mean that everyone needs to write a detailed business plan, though. While you should do some planning to figure out what direction you want to take your business, your plan could be as simple as a one-page business plan, or even a pitch presentation that highlights your current strategy."

Noah Parsons, "Key Business Plan Mistakes to Avoid in 2023", LivePlan, https://www.liveplan.com/blog/avoid-these-business-plan-mistakes/, 1/25/22

---

# 10 Tips to Craft a Successful Business Plan

All of this guidance is good, you say, but how does one pull all the content together into a successful plan? These ten tips will help:

1.  **Know your competition.** You need to name them and point out what makes you different from (and better than) each of them. But do not disparage your competition.

2.  **Know your audience.** You may need several versions of your business plan. For example, you may need one for bankers or venture capitalists, one for individual investors, and one for companies that may want to do a joint venture with you rather than fund you.

3.  **Have proof to back up every claim you make.** If you expect to be the leader in your field in six months, you have to say why you think that is. If you say your product will take the market by storm, you have to support this statement with facts. If you say your management team is fully qualified to make the business a success, be sure staff resumes demonstrate their experience.

4.  **Be conservative in all financial estimates and projections.** If you feel certain you'll capture 50 percent of the market in the first year, you can say why you think so and hint at what those numbers may be. But make your financial projections more conservative. For example, a 10 percent market share is much more credible.

5.  **Be realistic with time and resources available.** If you're working with a big company before you buy a business, you may think things will happen faster than they will once you have to buy the supplies, write the checks, and answer the phones yourself. Being overly optimistic with time and resources is a common error entrepreneurs make. Being realistic is important because it lends credibility to your presentation. Always assume things will take 20 percent longer than you anticipated. Therefore, twenty weeks is now twenty-four weeks.

6.  **Be logical.** Think like a banker and write what they would want to see.

7.  **Have a strong management team.** Make sure it has good credentials and expertise. Your team members don't have to have worked in the field. However, you need to draw parallels between what they've done and the skills needed to make your venture succeed. Don't

have all the skills you need? Consider adding an advisory board of people skilled in your field and include their resumes.

8. **Document why your idea will work.** Have others done something similar that was successful? Have you made a prototype? Include all the variables that can have an impact on the result or outcome of your idea. Show why some of the variables don't apply to your situation or explain how you intend to overcome them or make them better.

9. **Describe your facilities and location for performing the work.** That includes equipment you use to create your products and/or services. If you'll need to expand, discuss when, where, and why.

10. **Discuss payout options for the investors.** Some investors want a hands-on role. Some want to put associates on your board of directors. Some don't want to be involved in day-to-day activities at all. All investors want to know when they can get their money back and at what rate of return. Most want out within three to five years. Provide a brief description of options for investors, or at least mention that you're ready to discuss options with any serious prospect.

## Chapter 2 Summary

Business plans have a lot of elements in common, such as cash flow projections and marketing plans. And many of them share certain objectives as well, such as raising money or persuading a partner to join the firm. But all business plans are not the same any more than all businesses are.

Depending on your business and what you intend to use your plan for, you may need a very different type of business plan from what another entrepreneur needs. Plans differ widely in their length, detail of their contents, and the varying emphases they place on different aspects of the business.

What you'll learn from this chapter:

- How the industry you're in shapes your plan
- How your plan needs to present your business in the best light
- The four types of business plans
- Why you may want more than one business plan for different audiences

# One Plan Does Not Fit All

One of the reasons for differences among plans is that industries are different. A retailer isn't much like a manufacturer, and a professional-services firm isn't much like a fast-food restaurant. Each requires certain critical components for success—components that may be irrelevant or even completely absent in the operations of another type of firm.

For instance, inventory is a key concern of both retailers and manufacturers. Expert, innovative management of inventory is a very important part of the success of Walmart, one of the great all-time success stories in retail. Any business plan that purported to describe the important elements of these businesses would have had to devote considerable space to telling how the managers planned to manage inventory.

Contrast that with a professional-services firm, such as a management consultant. A consultant has no inventory whatsoever. Her offerings consist entirely of the management analysis and advice she and her staff can provide. She doesn't have to pay now for goods to be sold later or lay out cash to store products for eventual sale. The management consultant's business plan, therefore, wouldn't have a section on inventory or its management, control, and reduction.

This is just one pretty obvious example of the differences among plans for different industries. Sometimes even companies in more closely related industries have significantly different business plans. For instance, the business plan for a fine French restaurant might need a section detailing how the management intends to attract and retain a distinguished chef. At another restaurant, one catering to the downtown lunchtime crowd, a great deal of plan space might be devoted to the critical concern of location and quick turnaround of diners with very little about the chef.

If you are looking for extra guidance with an industry-specific business plan, you can visit Bplans.com (bplans.com/sample-business-plans/) to access over 500 free real-world business plan examples from a wide variety of industries to guide you through writing your own plan. If you're looking for an intuitive tool that walks you through the plan writing process, you can try LivePlan (liveplan.com/why-were-different). It includes many of these same SBA-approved business plan examples and is especially useful when applying for a bank loan or outside investment.

## Presenting Yourself in the Best Light

You want your plan to present yourself and your business in the best, most accurate light. That's true no matter what you intend to use your plan for, whether it's destined for presentation at a venture capital conference or will never leave your own office or be seen outside internal strategy sessions.

When you select clothing for an important occasion, odds are you try to pick items that will play up your best features. Think about your plan the same way. You want to reveal any positives that your business may have and make sure they receive due consideration.

## Your Plan Needs to Be Just Your Type

Business plans can be divided roughly into four distinct types. There are very short plans, or miniplans; presentation plans or decks; working plans; and what-if plans. They require very different amounts of labor and not always with proportionately different results. That is to say, a more elaborate plan is not guaranteed to be superior to an abbreviated one. Success depends on various factors and whether the right plan is used in the right setting. For example, a new hire may not want to read the same, elaborate version that might be important to a potential investor.

### The Miniplan

The miniplan is preferred by many recipients because they can read it or download it quickly to read later on their iPhone or tablet. You include most of the same ingredients that you would in a longer plan, but you cut to the highlights while telling the same story. For a small business venture, it's typically all that you need. For a more complex business, you may need the longer version.

### The Presentation Plan

The advent of PowerPoint presentations changed the way many, if not most, plans are presented. And while the plan is shorter than its predecessors, it's not necessarily easier to present. Many people lose sleep over an upcoming presentation, especially one that can play a vital role in the future of your business. And yet presenting your plan as a deck can be very powerful. Readers of a plan can't always capture your passion for the business, nor can they ask questions when you finish. In twenty minutes, you can cover all of the key points and tell your story from concept and mission statement through financial forecasts.

Remember to keep your graphics uncluttered and to make comments to accentuate your ideas rather than simply reading what is in front of your audience.

While a presentation plan is concise, don't be fooled. It takes plenty of planning. The pertinent questions—Who? What? Where? Why? When? and How?—need to be answered.

### A Guide to Your Deck: The 10–20–30 Plan

Using a deck is a quick, to-the-point means of providing your best-selling points while still sending over your more detailed plan.

The question is: How do you organize and minimize the breadth of a business plan into a PowerPoint presentation? First, it's recommended that you use the 10–20–30 rule, which means ten slides, twenty minutes, and a minimum of a 30-point font.

1. Your first slide is your title slide, which provides the name of the business, your name and title and contact information, plus a slogan if you have one. You can then read the slide and add, in a sentence, what it is you do.

2. The next slide should introduce a problem that persists and is relatable to your target market. Statistics can help you support your comments, but cite only a couple at best. You want the audience to relate to the problem or certainly understand how it affects others.

3. The third slide should get to your solution. Briefly describe in simple terms how your business has figured out how to alleviate the problem. Make sure the audience understands that you have a unique approach. You might also add a few words to support your overall value proposition.

4. Next you want to explain how you will make money. What are your revenue sources? Who are your customers? What is your pricing structure? Then talk briefly about how you expect to profit.

5. Now present a little more detail on your operating plan. How does it all work? Self-service? Kiosks? Personal service? Give them the short version of how the business operates. From buying the goods to marketing them, to sales and shipping, provide a short summary. Include a little technology—remember, "a little"! This is where you may need a second, visual slide to show how it all works.

6. Now it's time to present your marketing plan in a few short words. After all, if you're going to create dynamic advertising and promotional campaigns, what better way to start than briefly explaining how you plan to market the business? Give some specifics rather than saying "on the internet" or "on TV." Let your listeners know that you have a plan for marketing and can keep it within a reasonable budget.

7. Competition. Mention your key competitors—be nice. Then explain what gives you the competitive edge.

8. Talk about the team. Remember, people invest in other people. This is where you introduce your team, with a few very brief highlights (one line) of each member's background that relates to the business at hand.

9. Financials. This slide should show a clear projection with a three-to-five-year forecast. Explain the method you used to arrive at your numbers.

10. And finally, show them where you are at present. What have you done thus far, and how are you looking to move forward sooner rather than later? Present a positive call to action based on what you have accomplished to date and what you will accomplish in the future.

There are many ways to go about putting together your deck. And yes, if you need to go to twelve slides, do so, but try not to go longer.

A few tips:

▷ Don't talk in jargon; not everyone is deeply embedded in your industry.

▷ Don't post slides and then read them word for word. Your audience can read. Show something that is easy for them to digest and use your comments to provide a little deeper explanation. This way you present more information, some printed and some verbally.

- Take a breath between slides so you don't start motoring along.
- Do not focus on technology, technology, and more technology even if you are a tech company.
- Don't overload slides with too much material—people can only read and digest so much.
- Remember, less is more. Don't try to pack too much into a PowerPoint presentation so you can avoid the dreaded "PowerPoint poisoning" effect. Your listeners can always read the full plan for more details.

### The Working Plan

A working plan is a tool to be used to operate your business. It has to be long on detail but may be short on presentation. As with a miniplan, you probably can afford a somewhat higher degree of candor and informality when preparing a working plan. In a plan you intend to present to a bank loan committee, you might describe a rival as "competing primarily on a price basis." In a working plan, your comment about the same competitor might be, "When is Jones ever going to stop this insane price-cutting?"

A plan intended strictly for internal use may also omit some elements that you need not explain to yourself. Likewise, you probably don't need to include an appendix with resumes of key executives. Nor would a working plan especially benefit from product photos.

Internal policy considerations may guide the decision about whether to include or exclude certain information in a working plan. Many entrepreneurs are sensitive about employees knowing the precise salary the owner takes home from the business. To the extent such information can be left out of a working plan without compromising its utility, you can feel free to protect your privacy.

This document is like an old pair of khakis you wear to the office on Saturdays or that one ancient delivery truck that never seems to break down. It's there to be used, not admired.

We highly recommend growth planning to get the most from your business plan. It's an ongoing business planning process that combines the simplicity of the miniplan (or one-page plan) with the ongoing use and focus of the working plan. It just takes four simple steps:

> Create a plan: Quickly size up the potential of your idea, validate that it can be a real business, and set goals to make it work.
> Build your forecast: Develop an expense budget and financial projections to better understand where your business is now and where it is headed.
> Review the results: Compare your forecast against your actual sales and expenses each month to stay accountable and uncover new ideas.
> Refine your strategy: Adjust your business plan and forecast based on your learnings.

But, the goal of growth planning isn't to just produce documents that you use once and shelve. Instead, it helps you build a healthier company that will outlast all the business failure statistics.

It's faster than traditional business planning. You can complete an initial one-page plan that covers all of the necessary details about your business in just thirty minutes.

You can revise your plan and strategy in minutes instead of hours. This means that your plan stays up-to-date and useful for identifying potential problems and opportunities.

It's concise. Because growth planning requires you to document your ideas with limited text, your ideas are distilled to their core essence.

(Noah Parsons, "Growth Planning — The Modern Way to Write a Business Plan", LivePlan, https://www.liveplan.com/blog/growth-planning-process-explained/, 11/15/22)

## What-If Plans

When you face unusual circumstances, you need a variant on the working plan. For example, you might want to prepare a contingency plan when you are seeking bank financing. A contingency plan is a plan based on the worst-case scenario that you can imagine your business surviving—loss of market share, heavy price competition, defection of a key member of your management team. A contingency plan can soothe the fears of a banker or investor by demonstrating that you have indeed considered more than a rosy scenario.

Your business may be considering an acquisition, in which case a pro forma business plan (some call this a what-if plan) can help you understand what the acquisition is worth and how it might affect your core business. What if you raise prices, invest in staff training, and reduce duplicative efforts? Such what-if planning doesn't have to be as formal as a presentation plan. Perhaps you want to mull over the chances of a major expansion. A what-if plan can help you spot the increased needs for space, equipment, personnel, and other variables so you can make good decisions.

What sets these kinds of plans apart from the working and presentation plans is that they aren't necessarily describing how you will run the business. They are essentially more like an addendum to your actual business plan. If you decide to acquire that competitor or grow dramatically, you will want to incorporate some of the thinking already invested in these special purpose plans into your primary business plan.

## Your Presentation Counts

Just as fine dining locales offer finer sensory experiences than coffee shops or fast-food eateries, your presentation will differ from a working plan.

A working plan should be free from major errors, but a presentation plan must be proofread carefully several times by several people so that it is definitely free of grammatical errors or typos. You also may find inconsistencies in a working plan that you need to address as you move forward with your business planning. These must not exist in a plan ready for presentation.

It's also essential that a presentation plan be accurate. A mistake here could be construed as a misrepresentation by an unsympathetic outsider. At best, it will make you look less than careful. If the plan's summary describes a need for $40,000 in financing, but the cash flow projection shows $50,000 in financing coming in during the first year, you might think, "Oops! Forgot to update that summary to show the new numbers." The investor you're asking to pony up the cash, however, is unlikely to be so charitable.

### Think Visually

From infographics to YouTube, we are clearly embracing visuals and graphics as never before. Depending on your industry and the software you are using, it may be in your best interest to utilize graphics to enhance the presentation of any business plan. If, for example, you are in the fashion, food, or design industry or you are creating a new product, your visual image will certainly be worth a thousand words. The key is to choose the best graphics and insert them appropriately—keep in mind that any visual must fit into the plan. Don't overdo it. Consider the impact visuals are having in marketing where studies show that people are much more likely to remember any type of presentation or advertisement with visuals than those without.

You can also provide plan readers with information and even apps to look at what it is you are proposing. Having everyone in the room on the same page, literally, can allow them to utilize interactive features and help you display any new technology that factors into your business operations.

"Not only does our brain process visual information so much more effectively than text, but visuals are also simply more persuasive.

A 3M-sponsored study found that presenters who use visual aids are 43 percent more effective in getting people to do what they want.

Imagine that you're trying to get funding for your business and that your presentation could be that much more effective if it presents data visually instead of with text. I'll bet that any entrepreneur would take advantage of that fact if they knew the statistics were that much in their favor."

Noah Parsons, "Do Visuals Really Trump Text?", LivePlan, https://www.liveplan.com/blog/scientific-reasons-why-you-should-present-your-data-visually/, 6/14/18

## Why You May Want More Than One Plan

So you've looked over the different types of plans. Which one is for you? Odds are that you'll need more than one variety. If you want to get maximum impact from your plan, you'll need to tailor it to address the particular needs of each potential audience.

### Target Audiences

The potential readers of a business plan are a varied bunch, ranging from bankers and venture capitalists to employees. Although this is a diverse group, it is a finite one. And each type of reader does have certain typical interests. If you know these interests up front, you can be sure to take them into account when preparing a plan for that particular audience.

Active venture capitalists see hundreds of plans in the course of a year. Most plans probably receive no more than a glance from a given venture capitalist before being rejected; others get just a cursory inspection. Even if your plan excites initial interest, it may receive only a few minutes of attention to begin with. It's essential, when courting these harried investors, that you make the right impression fast. Emphasize a cogent, succinct summary and explanation of the basic business concept, and do not stint on the details about the impressive backgrounds of your management team. That said, make it concise and to the point. Remember, time is of the essence to venture capitalists and other investors.

Bankers tend to be more formal than venture capitalists and more concerned with financial strength than with exciting concepts and impressive resumes. For these readers, you'll want to give extra attention to balance sheets and cash flow statements. Make sure they're fully detailed and come with notes to explain any anomalies or possible points of confusion.

Angel investors may not insist on seeing a plan at all, but as we pointed out in Chapter 2, your responsibilities as a businessperson require you to show them one anyway. For such an informal investor, prepare a less formal plan. Rather than going for impressive bulk, seek brevity. An angel investor used to playing her hunches might be put off by an imposing plan rather than impressed with your thoroughness.

If you were thinking about becoming a partner in a firm, you'd no doubt be very concerned with the responsibilities you would have, the authority you would carry, and the ownership you would receive in the enterprise. Naturally, anyone who is considering partnering with you is going to have similar concerns. So make sure that any plan presented to a potential partner deals comprehensively with the ownership structure and clearly spells out matters of control and accountability.

Customers who are looking at your business plan are probably doing so because they contemplate building a long-term relationship with you. They are certainly going to be more concerned about your relationships with your other customers and, possibly, suppliers than most of your readers. So deal with these sections of your plan in greater depth, but you can be more concise in other areas. Customers rarely ever read a company's business plan, so you'll probably have your miniplan available for these occasions.

Suppliers have a lot of the same concerns as customers, except they're in the other direction on the supply chain. They'll want, above all, to make sure you can pay your bills, so be sure to include adequate cash flow forecasts and other financial reports. Suppliers, who naturally would like their customers to order more and more, are likely to be quite interested in your growth prospects. In fact, if you can show you're probably going to be growing a lot, you may be in a better position to negotiate terms with your suppliers. Like customers, most suppliers do not take the time to read lengthy business plans, so again, focus on the shorter version for such purposes.

Strategic allies usually come to you for something specific—technology, distribution, complementary customer sets, and so on. So any plan you show to a potential ally will stress this aspect of your operation. Sometimes potential strategic partners may also be potential competitors, so you may want to present your plan in stages, saving sensitive information such as financials and marketing strategies for later in the process when trust has been established.

---

### ⟫ plan pointer

Instead of writing a whole new plan for each audience, construct a modular plan with interchangeable sections. Pull out the resume section for internal use, for example, and plug it back in for presentation to an investor. A modular, mix-and-match plan saves time and effort while preserving flexibility. Many people do this with resumes: They have sections that they include or take out depending on the job for which they are applying.

---

Managers in your company are using the plan primarily to remind themselves of objectives, to keep strategies clear, and to monitor company performance and market conditions. You'll want to stress such things as corporate mission and vision statements and analyses of current industry and economic factors. The most important part of a plan intended for management consumption is probably in the financials. You'll want to take special care to make it easy for managers to compare sales revenue, profitability, and other key financial measures against planned performance.

There's one caution to the plan-customization exercise. Limit your alterations from one plan to another to modifying the emphasis of the information you present. Don't show one set of numbers to a banker you're trying to borrow money from and another to a partner you're trying to lure on board. It's one thing to stress one aspect of your operation over another for presentation purposes and entirely another to distort the truth.

## Include Investments

If you are already invested in the stock market, bonds, or even more directly in other businesses, you should let this be clearly known in your business plan. This provides readers with

> ⟩ an understanding that you are somewhat versed in matters of investing
> ⟩ your level of risk tolerance, based on your investments
> ⟩ your plans for growth or ability to raise capital depending on your choices of investments

Investing indicates that you are planning ahead and looking to make profits either through long-term growth or through dividends and other income-producing investment vehicles. Personal investments and, of course, business investments are important to readers as they paint a picture of how you will handle financing.

## Chapter 3 Summary

You've decided to write a business plan, and you're ready to get started. Congratulations. You've just greatly increased the chances that your business venture will succeed. But before you draft your plan, you need to focus on several areas from conceptual to "concrete." One of the most important reasons to plan your plan is that you are accountable for the projections and proposals it contains. That's especially true if you use your plan to raise money to finance your company.

Business plans can be complicated documents. You'll be making lots of decisions as you draft your plan, on serious matters, such as what strategy you'll pursue, as well as less important ones like what color paper to print it on. Thinking about these decisions in advance is an important way to minimize the time you spend planning and to maximize the time you spend generating income.

What you'll learn from this chapter:

- » How to determine your business goals and objectives
- » How you will finance your business
- » What the purpose of your business is
- » The software you need to create your business plan

# Line Up Your Ducks

Close your eyes. Imagine that it's five years from now. Where do you want to be? What will the business look like? Will you be running a business that hasn't increased significantly in size? Will you command a rapidly growing empire? Will you have already cashed out and be relaxing on a beach somewhere, enjoying your hard-won gains?

Now is a good time to free-associate a little bit—let your mind roam, exploring every avenue that you would like your business to go down. Try writing a personal essay on your business goals. It could take the form of a letter to yourself, written from five years in the future, describing all you have accomplished and how it came about.

As you read such a document, you may make a surprising discovery, such as that you don't really want to own a large, fast-growing enterprise but would be content with a stable small business. Even if you don't learn anything new, getting a firm handle on your goals and objectives is a big help in deciding how you'll plan your business. Answering the questions in Figure 3.1 is an important part of building a successful business plan. If you don't have a destination in mind, it's not possible to plan at all.

>>> **buzzword**

Goals: Business goals are typically long-term calculated plans that you are working toward. They may encompass one or several shorter objectives and can be measured along the way, often by setting up milestones. Goals should be realistic and include a time frame.

## What Are Your Goals and Objectives?

If you're having trouble deciding what your goals and objectives are, here are some questions to ask yourself.

1. How determined am I to see this venture succeed?
2. Am I willing to invest my own money and to work long hours for no pay, sacrificing personal time and lifestyle, maybe for years?
3. What's going to happen to me if this venture doesn't work?
4. If it does succeed, how many employees will this company eventually have?
5. What will be its annual sales in a year? Five years?
6. What will be its market share in that time frame?
7. Will it be a niche market, or will it sell a broad spectrum of goods and services?
8. What are the plans for geographic expansion? Local? National? Global?
9. Am I going to be a hands-on manager, or will I delegate a large proportion of tasks to others?

10. If I delegate, what sorts of tasks will I share? Sales? Technical? Others?

11. How comfortable am I taking direction from others? Could I work with partners or investors who demand input into the company's management?

12. Is this venture going to remain independent and privately owned, or will it eventually be acquired or go public?

**Figure 3.1.** What Are Your Goals and Objectives?

Your plan may look beautiful, but without a solid understanding of your own intentions in business, it is likely to lack coherence and, ultimately, prove ineffective. Let's say in one section you describe a mushrooming enterprise on a fast-growth track, then elsewhere endorse a strategy of slow and steady expansion. Any business plan reader worth his or her salt is going to be bothered by inconsistencies like these. They suggest that you haven't thought through your intentions. Avoid inconsistency by deciding in advance what your goals and objectives will be and sticking with them.

## Focus on Financing

It doesn't necessarily take a lot of money to make a lot of money, but it does take some. That's especially true if, as part of examining your goals and objectives, you envision very rapid growth.

Energetic, optimistic entrepreneurs tend to believe that sales growth will take care of everything, that they will be able to fund their own growth by generating profits. However, this is rarely the case, for one simple reason: You usually have to pay your own suppliers **before** your customers pay you. This cash flow conundrum is the reason so many fast-growing companies have to seek bank financing or sell equity to finance their growth. They are growing faster than they can afford.

Sometimes the cash flow gap is very large. Pharmaceutical companies may spend hundreds of millions of dollars in a multiyear project to develop and bring to market a new drug. These companies must have large cash flows from other products to fill the gap or seek loans or other forms of financing to avoid running out of money before having a market-ready product.

> You need to understand the financial implications of your decisions. Because the only reason you go out of business is that you run out of money. You run out of cash. You owe people money. You go bankrupt. You fail.
>
> Even though the reasons for failure can be related to marketing, implementation, supply change, fulfillment, or just an overall economic slowdown, the proof is in the numbers.
>
> If you can manage those numbers and understand what lower sales are going to do to your cost structure, or if you understand areas where maybe you can become leaner without affecting your core business, you're going to be able to get through tough times.
>
> You're going to position yourself to be able to grow in healthier ways because you will be very aware of all the levers that drive your business.
>
> Sabrina Parsons, "How We Made It Through a Recession, Became a Subscription-Oriented Business, and Stayed Cash Flow Positive", LivePlan, https://www.liveplan.com/blog/how-to-stay-cash-flow-positive-when-times-get-tough/, 3/12/20

#### ⫸ buzzword

Objectives: In business, objectives are specific results you are seeking to achieve within a specific time. They are usually short term and are easily measurable. Minimizing expenses, increasing revenue, and rolling out a new product are examples of objectives. They can also help you meet long-term goals.

**Low-Budget Businesses**

You can start a very low-budget business and write a business plan as it evolves to bring in capital for advertising, marketing, and/or expansion. Many service businesses revolve primarily around using your time, motivation, knowledge, ingenuity, communication skills, and other factors that do not necessitate much outlay of funds. Consultants, counselors, coaches, cleaning services, web designers, writers, organizers, and many other possible businesses can be started by you, in your home, with very little funding.

The main cost will be promoting what you do, and much of that can be done online and by word of mouth. Websites are inexpensive to build, and once you get started you can put your initial income back into the business for a while. Then, when you have a list of clients and even some testimonials from them, you can begin working on your business plan to build up your business.

Other companies require much smaller amounts of capital to finance their ongoing operations. Small service firms such as local web-design companies or carpet cleaners frequently operate on a cash basis, getting paid with cash, check, or credit card at the time they perform their services after making only small outlays for supplies in advance. But as a general rule, your business will most likely have to consider some kind of financing, as discussed in the next chapter. Now is the time to think about some of the issues that will surface.

Start by asking yourself what kinds of financing you are likely to need—and what you'd be willing to accept. It's easy when you're short of cash, or expect to be short of cash, to take the attitude that almost any source of funding is just fine. But each kind of financing has different characteristics that you should take into consideration when planning your future. These characteristics take three primary forms.

>>> **plan of action**

Many enterprises can be started with the help of modest amounts of cash, no more than the contents of a small savings account. Here are some good places to find business ideas that can spark your own:

- Entrepreneur.com, which has plenty of ideas, resources, and more. It's a great supplement to this book.
- The Springwise website (https://www.springwise.com/) has plenty of business ventures and ideas, and the site categorizes these ideas by industry.
- The HubSpot blog (https://blog.hubspot.com/sales/small-business-ideas) has sixty ideas for starting your own business.
- The Shopify e-commerce blog (https://www.shopify.com/blog/unique-business-ideas) has seventeen business ideas of their own.

Don't forget that you can also get a lot of startup business ideas in *Start Your Own Business: The Only Startup Book You'll Ever Need* (Entrepreneur Press) by the Staff of Entrepreneur Media, Inc.

First, there's the amount of control you'll have to surrender. An equal-equity partner may, quite naturally, demand approximately equal control. Venture capitalists often demand significant input into management decisions by placing one or more people on your board of directors. Angel investors may be very involved or not involved at all, depending on personal style. Bankers, at the other end of the scale, are likely to offer no advice whatsoever as long as you make payments of principal and interest on time and are not in violation of any other terms of your loan. Second, consider the amount of money you are likely to need. This means carefully considering your startup needs as well as your ongoing operational needs projected for several years.

Once you have determined whether you can launch and run a business for $20,000, $200,000, $2 million, or $200 million, you will be able to consider the various funding sources. You may need to consider several funding sources. See Figure 3.2 for comparisons.

Almost any source of funds, from a bank to a venture capital firm, has some guidelines about the size of financing it prefers. Anticipating the size of your needs now will guide you in preparing your plan.

The third consideration is cost. This can be measured in terms of interest rates and shares of ownership, as well as in time, paperwork, and plain old hassle. At the top of the list are public offerings of stock, which may cost several hundred thousand dollars in legal and accounting fees to put together and require a great deal of your own time and attention.

| Financing Source | Control | Funds | Cost |
| --- | --- | --- | --- |
| Friends & family | Varies | Usually small | Low or none |
| Bank loan | Little | Varies | Varies |
| Partner | Potentially large | Varies | Low |
| Government-backed loan | Little | Usually small | Low |
| Venture capital | Large | Moderate to large | Low |
| Angel investor | Varies | Small to moderate | Low |
| Stock offering | Large | Large | Large |

More on these forms of financing will show up in the next chapter.

Figure 3.2. Financing Characteristics Comparison

## What's Your Purpose?

Your business plan can be used for several things, from monitoring your company's progress toward goals to enticing key employees to join your firm. Deciding how you intend to use yours is an important part of preparing to write it.

> ⟩ *Do you intend to use your plan to help raise money?* In that case, you'll have to focus very carefully on the executive summary, management, and marketing and financial aspects. You'll need to have a clearly focused vision of how your company is going to make money. If you're looking for a bank loan, you'll need to stress your ability to generate sufficient cash flow to service loans. Equity investors, especially venture capitalists, must be shown how they can cash out of your company and generate a rate of return they'll find acceptable.

> ⟩ *Do you intend to use your plan to attract talented employees?* Then you'll want to emphasize such things as stock options and other aspects of compensation, as well as location, work environment, corporate culture, and opportunities for growth and advancement. If you're a high-tech startup, top employees are likely to ask to see your plans for attracting venture capital and later selling out to a bigger firm or going public so they can realize the value of their stock options.

> ⟩ *Do you anticipate showing your plan to suppliers to demonstrate that you are a worthy customer?* A solid business plan may convince a supplier of some precious commodity to favor you over your rivals. It may also help you to arrange supplier credit—one of the most useful forms of financing to a small business. You may want to stress your blue-ribbon customer list and spotless record of repaying trade debts in this plan.

> ⟩ *Do you hope to convince big customers that you will be a dependable supplier?* Then you'll want to emphasize your staying power, innovation, and special capabilities. In this plan, unlike the supplier-targeted one, you may want to play down relationships with other big customers, especially if they are foes of the one you're wooing.

**buzzword**

Working capital is the amount of money a business has in cash, accounts receivable, inventory, and other current assets. (Current assets are assets likely to be turned into cash within a year.) Net working capital, which is what this term usually refers to, is current assets minus current liabilities. (Current liabilities are things like accounts payable to suppliers and short-term loans due in less than a year.) The higher the amount of net working capital you require, the greater your financing needs are likely to be.

## When Is a Negative a Positive?

Cash is one of the major constraints on the growth of any business. It's the reason why even highly profitable, fast-growing companies frequently have to go hat in hand to borrowers, seeking money to allow them to fill their orders so they can turn sales into cash. There's one type of company, however, that doesn't have a problem with cash. It's one with a negative cash conversion cycle, which means a company collects the cash several days before having to pay its suppliers.

Netflix is an example of a company working with a negative cash flow conversion cycle. The company had to keep lifting its cash outlays on new programming more quickly than it expensed spending as amortization on its income statement. Not many businesses have the success and reputation to make something like this work.

›  *Do you expect to use your plan only for internal purposes?* Then you'll want to build in many milestones, benchmarks, and other tools for measuring and comparing your future performance against the plan. Such things may be of little interest to a banker evaluating your loan-worthiness but could make all the difference between a useful plan and one that's no good at all for monitoring corporate performance.

These distinctions are not merely academic. A plan that's well suited for internal purposes would probably be completely wrong for taking to a potential Fortune 500 customer. Actually, the marketplace of business plan consumers is even more finely segmented than that. A plan for a bank, for instance, wouldn't accomplish much by including a strategy for selling the company to a large conglomerate several years down the road, whereas a venture capitalist would look for your exit strategy very early on.

Think about all this and keep it in mind as you create your plan. Along the way, you'll have to make many decisions about what to include or leave out and what to stress or play down. Setting some direction now about how you intend to use your plan will make those later decisions faster and more accurate.

Because many entrepreneurs utilize business plans for various purposes, you'll want to have several versions available. By carefully editing and rewriting certain sections with your audience in mind, you can have plans ready for different occasions. The plan for raising funding will likely be more extensive and detailed than the plan for attracting new employees, who may not want to read as much but will want some answers to the question, Why should I work at your company? While the business plan is the sum of various sections, how you massage and edit those sections can help you utilize it for a variety of purposes.

Consider that once you've created a good business plan, you should use it in as many ways as possible, including self-motivation and guidance as you make business decisions and undergo changes.

>>> **buzzword**

Cash conversion cycle is an arcane financial measure that is a powerful indicator of a business's health. It represents the time it takes to transform outlays into income. For a manufacturer, that means the number of days required to purchase raw material and turn it into inventory, then sales, and, finally, collections. The shorter your cash conversion cycle, the better.

## Get the Software You Need

Now that you've thought about your goals, focused on your financing, and determined the purpose of your plan (and considered to whom you will send it), you'll want to take a practical approach and consider some of the software tools of the trade.

While you remain in the driver's seat, writing the plan and doing all the heavy thinking, your business plan software can handle research, organization, calculations, and more.

Of course, you don't have to use specific business plan software to write your plan. Microsoft Office or any similar software on which you can write each section of your plan can serve your purpose. You can even use Excel, Google Sheets, or other spreadsheet software to handle the financial pages.

However, should you want the guidance of a software program, you'll want to find one that meets your computer capabilities, has tech support readily available, and is highly rated. You should also ask other business owners, perhaps in your local chamber of commerce, which ones they used and what they have to say about the software.

Looking at https://www.capterra.com/business-plan-software/, you'll find product comparisons, including research tools provided, printing and publishing, support, and more. Look the plans over and decide which one has what you need.

For a tool that helps you manage and grow your business even past that initial starting phase, you can try out LivePlan. When asked what stands them apart, LivePlan says, "While other business planning apps become irrelevant once your plan is complete — that's just the beginning with

LivePlan. Goal tracking, performance dashboards, and forecast scenarios will empower you to confidently answer important questions like, 'How can I use this funding to help my business?' 'Where should I invest my marketing to grow?' and 'What happens if I have a bad month?'"

---

### ≫ plan pitfall

Thanks to plan-writing software's built-in financial formulas, you just have to plug in the data. Because you don't enter the formulas yourself, however, you won't have the same understanding of your financial statements as if you had to think about and manually enter them. So, if you use plan-writing software, look under the hood and see what is going on inside all those spreadsheets.

---

The functionality of the software and how much instruction is provided are key to making an informed decision. Many have the same or similar features, but those that you can learn without tearing your hair out are the best choices. The latest in software is designed to walk you through the process. However, some walk you more directly while others walk you in a circle before getting you to where you want to go. Do your research.

The bottom line with software, however, is that it can only provide what you ask for. Too often, people misunderstand the capabilities of software. Remember, it cannot write the business plan for you.

Among the various software options, three of the more popular programs to consider are LivePlan, Bizplan, and Enloop.

### Chapter 4 Summary

Abusiness plan is almost essential for entrepreneurs seeking to raise money to help fund their companies. In fact, business plans are so closely tied to fundraising that many entrepreneurs look at them as suited only for presenting to investors and overlook the management benefits of planning. But for those entrepreneurs who are seeking funding, a business plan accomplishes several things. First, it helps convince potential sources of funding that the entrepreneur has thought the idea through. It also gives any actual investors a set of financial benchmarks for which the entrepreneur can be held accountable.

In a sense, a business plan is a ticket to enter the financial dance. It would be overly simplistic to say that you must have a plan to get funding. But it's not too simplistic to say that a good plan will help you raise your funds more quickly, more easily, and more completely than you could without it.

What you'll learn from this chapter:

 » How to justify the ideas in your plan
 » How to assess your company's potential for growth
 » How to find direct funding sources
 » Where you can find indirect funding sources

# Digging for Dollars

## Justification of Your Ideas

Before seeking investors, you need to know exactly what you are seeking and where that money will be spent. Not unlike justifying expenses when sending your taxes to the IRS, you need to justify the amounts you are asking for and be specific. Investors are not simply writing out checks with no idea of where the money will be spent. Sure, you can ask for a little more than you need in hopes that the negotiating brings you down to the amount you truly need for funding . . . or something reasonably close. It's also important to maintain your credibility because you will probably need additional funding as your company grows. Therefore, if you squander the money your investors have provided, you can be pretty sure you won't get a round two when you need additional funding.

Having justification for what you put in your plan is essential for winning over someone reading it. Random ideas get random results. Well-thought-out, justified ideas get serious consideration.

---

"The business plan document itself isn't what's important to investors. It's the knowledge that you've generated by going through the process that's important. Having a business plan shows that you've done the homework of thinking through how your business will work and what goals you're trying to achieve.

When you put together a business plan, you have to spend time thinking about things like your target market, your sales, and marketing strategy, the problem you solve for your customers, and who your key competitors are. A business plan provides the structure for thinking through these things and documents your answers so you're prepared for the inevitable questions investors will ask about your business.

Even if investors never ask to see your business plan, the work you've done to prepare it will ensure that you can intelligently answer the questions you'll get. And, if an investor does ask for your business plan, then you're prepared and ready to hand it over. After all, nothing could be worse than arriving at an investor meeting and then getting a request for a business plan and not having one ready."

(Noah Parsons, "How to Write a Convincing Business Plan for Investors", Bplans, https://articles.bplans.com/write-business-plan-for-investors/, 2/10/21)

---

## Assessing Your Company's Potential

It's also advantageous to take a few minutes to make sure that your company has the potential to succeed before digging for those hard-to-get dollars. For most of us, our desires about where we would like to go are not as important as our businesses' ability to take us there. Put another way, if you choose the wrong business, you're going nowhere.

Luckily, one of the most valuable uses of a business plan is to help you decide whether the venture you have your heart set on is really likely to fulfill your dreams. Many, many businesses never make it past the planning stage because their would-be founders, as part of a logical and coherent planning process, test their assumptions and find them wanting.

Test your idea against at least two variables. First, financial, to make sure this business makes economic sense. Second, lifestyle, because who wants a successful business that they hate? Figure 4.1 can help you focus on your financial and lifestyle goals.

> "Investors want more than just an idea. They want evidence that you are solving a problem for customers. Your customers have to want what you are selling for you to build a successful business and your business plan needs to describe the evidence that you've found that proves that you'll be able to sell your products and services to customers. If you have "traction" in the form of early sales and customers, that's even better."
>
> (Noah Parsons, "How to Write a Convincing Business Plan for Investors", Bplans, https://articles.bplans.com/write-business-plan-for-investors/, 2/10/21)

## Assessing Your Company's Potential

Answer the following questions to help you outline your company's potential. There are no wrong answers. The objective is simply to help you decide how well your proposed venture is likely to match your goals and objectives.

### Financial

1.  What initial investment will the business require?
2.  How much control are you willing to relinquish to investors?
3.  When will the business turn a profit?
4.  When can investors, including you, expect a return on their money?
5.  What are the projected profits of the business over time?
6.  Will you be able to devote yourself full-time to the business financially?
7.  What kind of salary or profit distribution can you expect to take home?
8.  What are the chances the business will fail?
9.  What will happen if it does?
10. Do you have a backup or alternative plan?

**Figure 4.1.** Assessing Your Company's Potential

---

### Tips to Help You Win Funding

Keep these tips in mind to help you win the funding you are searching for:

▷ Spend extra time working on the executive summary. (See Chapter 6.) Because bankers and professional investors receive so many business plans, they sometimes go right to the executive summary for an overall view of what your plan is all about. If you can't seize their interest in your executive summary, go back to the drawing board and try again.

> Make sure your business plan is complete. You would be surprised at how many business plans are submitted with important data missing. You need to double- and triple-check to make sure all of the important components are included. Even when using business plan software, people skip sections or decide an area is not important. Leave nothing to chance. A well-written and complete business plan gives you a higher chance of success and better odds of getting the financing you are seeking.

> Be able to back up anything you have on paper if asked for more details. While the business plan should have all the answers, investors, bankers, and venture capitalists are shrewd and ask questions that may not be answered in the plan. Be ready to answer anything they can possibly throw at you. Expect the unexpected and prepare for it.

So, when you assess your company's potential, what are you and your readers supposed to learn from answering these questions?

- If you can devote the time you need to grow your business full-time.
- How much money you need to start the business so that you know if you have enough money already or how much you need to raise from outside sources to make your dream a reality.
- If you're willing to give up some control to investors, or you prefer to bootstrap financing of the business with your own money as well as friends and family if they're willing.
- Understand how your business will make money and how you will pay yourself, your employees, and your investors.
- What plans you will put in motion if the business shows signs of failure.

## Direct Funding Sources

When you're looking for money, it may seem that investors are scarce. But the real problem may be that you're not looking in enough places for potential financiers. You may find investors as close as your immediate family and as far away as professional venture capitalists on the other side of the world.

Investors come in many shapes and sizes, as well as with various needs and intentions. Odds are you can find someone to help you with your financing needs if you cast your net wide enough.

### *Your Own Resources*

Your own resources, savings, investments, and other valuable assets are the beginning of your financing efforts. One reason to write a business plan is to provide reassurance that you are making a sensible investment. Note that you will be investing serious nonfinancial assets in your business: your time, effort, hopes, and reputation.

As for your own financial assets, make sure the money is not earmarked for tuition or part of your necessary family spending, such as your mortgage, rent, and the like. If you're in debt, it is also advisable to get out from under before starting a business. But you can start writing your business plan while getting your financial affairs in order.

Even though hopefully you will be investing assets from investors, you should be prepared to invest some of your own money in your business venture. Rule of thumb says if you want other people to invest in you, then you also have to invest in yourself.

Why should other people take a gamble on your business if you won't?

### *Friends and Family*

The most likely source of financing is the group of people closest to you. Spouses, parents, grandparents, aunts, uncles, and in-laws, as well as friends and colleagues, have reasons to help you that arm's-length financiers lack. For that reason, they may back you when no one else will.

One seldom-noticed aspect of asking family and friends to invest in your venture is that other investors (especially bankers and venture capitalists) often ask if you have approached friends and family to raise initial capital. If you say you haven't, they'll then ask why not. If your deal is so appealing, why wouldn't you let your friends in on the ground floor? If you say yes, but they couldn't come through for you, at least the banker or VC will know you tried.

Willingness to take a risk doesn't make friends and family foolish investors. Money from family and friends has backed many very successful business ventures. Here are a few:

> ⟫ Albertson's Inc. Cofounder Joe Albertson borrowed $7,500 from his aunt to make his $12,500 contribution to the partnership that began the grocery store that grew to have sales of more than $2 billion a year.
> ⟫ Pizza Hut Inc. Cofounders Frank and Dan Carney borrowed $600 from an insurance fund left by their late father to start the pizza chain.
> ⟫ Eckerd Corporation. Jack Eckerd raised $150,000 from family members to purchase three failing Florida drugstores, the cornerstone of a company whose sales would one day top $9 billion a year.

Friends and family may not be able to raise millions of dollars, but they can provide long-term financing for highly speculative endeavors that more mainstream financiers wouldn't touch.

---

### ⟫⟫ buzzword

Direct funding sources invest directly in your business. These include funds from individuals, banks, government agencies, and various levels of professional investors. Indirect funding sources provide trade credit and financing mechanisms such as extended terms on purchases. These are important sources of working capital, but they do not put funds directly into your business.

---

## Even Families Need a Plan

If you're financing your venture with family money, you may think all you need is a smile and a polite request to raise what you need. In the short term, that may work and produce the funds you need to start out. But over the long term, even family financed enterprises will benefit from having a business plan.

Such a plan shows family members who are putting up the money what they can expect for their contribution. And it helps keep the entrepreneur—you—mindful of responsibilities to the family members who backed you and on track to fulfill your obligations.

> Chief Financial Officer Trevor Betenson of Palo Alto Software (makers of LivePlan) finds that funding your business through the help of friends and family can be a great opportunity—as long as you take the necessary steps to protect both parties. He says,"If you're doing friends and family financing, you have got to make sure that you're still treating it like it is a real thing. You can't just have someone hand you a check and then you give a handshake agreement. You still need to make sure you have a lawyer look at it, ideally. Have documents drawn up, [and] have something notarized. That way you're treating it as if it were a bank or someone more professional giving you a loan. What you don't want to have happen is later down the line there is a question [or] a concern—you don't want to ruin relationships," (Betenson, Trevor. Interview. Conducted by Makenna Crocker. 28 February 2023.)

### *Pros and Cons of Family Funding*

On the positive side, family and friends will let you know if your idea appeals to them. Typically, they will also give you the time and a less stressful environment in which to present your plan. Family members may be more readily available to lend a helping hand when you need one and may be there to take over the business down the road.

The flip side is that you are closer to your family and friends. Losing the money of someone close to you can create a lot of tension between you and your family or friends. Family members and friends may also want to get more involved and try to oversee aspects of the business or push you to make changes that other investors would not. They may even expect to be on your management team, which would not be the case with a bank.

In order to make investor agreements work with friends and family, you need to spell out everything clearly and make sure you can separate your business from your personal relationships. This is not necessarily as easy as it sounds. You need to go into any such deals playing some defense and making it clear that people may lose their investments. Provide plenty of warning, and, if they insist on being part of your business, make sure there are boundaries set out in advance that everyone can agree upon.

### Crowdfunding

A rather recent entry into the world of procuring funds for projects is crowdfunding. This is a means of gathering funds from a diverse group of investors using internet technology.

The idea is broad based with some investors on crowdfunding sites getting rewards for investing money while others become investors with a stake in the business. As a result, some of these sites are, like PBS, seeking support from generous people with a passion for a type of business or short-term project or for a cause behind that business or project. Other sites are looking for investors in more full-blown long-term business ventures.

Statista, a leading provider of market and consumer data, reported that the overall industry raised more than $13.6 billion in 2021, and is forecast to more than double to nearly $29 billion in 2028.

---

### ▷▷ plan pitfall

Family members offer tempting capital sources. But emotions can interfere with judgment when dealing with relatives and can lead to hurt feelings as well as possible lawsuits and other entanglements. Minimize the risk of such misunderstandings by fully documenting terms, possible interest rates, and other details for loans and equity investments from family.

If you do not document the terms of such loans in writing, the IRS can either treat the loan as permanent capital or impute a stiff interest rate to the loan. Neither of these options is desirable.

---

Adam Chapnick, former head of Indiegogo, notes that an abbreviated business plan works best for most crowdfunding sites. "Make a big fat business plan—then throw it away," says Chapnick, adding that it is important to go through the process of creating a business plan and then necessary to simplify it and make it quick to convey for crowdfunding.

MicroVentures starts off with a snapshot questionnaire to which you can attach a business plan if you so choose, but it's not required. Like Indiegogo, it would also look for the abridged version of your longer plan.

There are more crowdfunding services coming of age, with new parameters and guidelines, many of which meet specific niche groups. Rules are changing, in part because of federal and SEC regulations and in part because the crowdfunding services are seeing new ways of doing business. For example, Kickstarter, the early trendsetter in this industry, which has raised over $300 million for over 1,800 projects, will give the new business venture the money that has been raised only if the total amount requested has been reached. Therefore, if you request $10,000 to start a business, and you raise only $7,500 from interested parties, you get nothing. Other services, though, would give you the $7,500. Kickstarter is also more selective about what projects end up on its website, looking for more "trendy" ideas to keep the company in the limelight.

By reviewing the various crowdfunding websites, you can determine which one might be best for your efforts. Look at what the investors will get in return. This can be anything from a gift, not unlike pledging money to PBS; a return on the investment with interest; or, on equity investment crowdfunding websites, a share in the business.

Also keep in mind that many people invest in crowdfunding ventures with their hearts and/or emotions. It is a daring means of investing, but one that drives many crowdfunding investors to put money into something in which they personally believe, such as an environmentally sound business.

Of course, there are downsides to crowdfunding, such as putting an idea out there that can be easily stolen or having backers that offer money only while not giving you either the network you need, good business advice, or second rounds of funding. There is also a lot of time spent on marketing to raise your funds. In addition, the SEC is closely watching this new investment opportunity, so you need to be abreast of the latest rules governing crowdfunding.

While Kickstarter and Indiegogo are more frequently used for creative projects, business owners have found success with AngelList.com, MicroVentures.com, or CircleUp.com. But there are so many more that you can find by searching online for "crowdfunding for business."

### Banks

Many of the most successful businesses are financed by banks, which can provide small to moderate amounts of capital at market costs. They don't want control—at least beyond the control exerted in the covenants of a loan document. And they don't want ownership. Bankers make loans, not investments, and as a general rule they don't want to wind up owning your company.

Bankers primarily provide debt financing. You take out a loan and pay it back, perhaps in installments consisting of principal and interest, perhaps in payments of interest only, followed by a balloon payment of the principal. One of the nice things about debt financing is that the entrepreneur doesn't have to give up ownership of his company to get it. The cost is clearly stated.

Bankers can usually be counted on to want minimal, if any, input into how the business is run. Most often, as long as you remain current on payments, you can do as you like. Get behind on the payment schedule, and you're likely to find a host of covenants buried in your loan documentation.

Loan covenants, however, may require you to do all sorts of things, from setting a minimum amount of working capital you must maintain to prohibiting you from making certain purchases or signing leases without approval from the bank. In fact, most bank loans contain so many covenants that it's difficult for a borrower to avoid being technically in default on one or more of them at a given time. For this reason, you want your accountant, financial advisor, or attorney to review your loan documents and spell out everything for you very carefully.

Your loan officer is likely to ignore many covenant violations unless you stop, or seem likely to stop, making timely payments. Even then you'll probably get a chance to work out the problem. But if you remain in violation, you may find yourself declared in default in short order, and the bank may demand all of its money immediately, perhaps seizing your collateral and even forcing you to protect yourself by declaring bankruptcy.

## What Bankers Want

A banker's first concern is getting the bank's money back plus a reasonable return. To increase the odds of this, bankers look for certain things in the businesses they lend to. Those include everything from a solid explanation of why you need the money and what you're going to use it for to details about any other borrowing or leasing deals you've entered into.

Bank loan applications can be voluminous, almost as long and complete as a full-fledged business plan. Plans and loan applications aren't interchangeable, however. A banker may not be interested in your rosy projections of future growth. In fact, when confronted with the kind of growth projection required to interest a venture capitalist, a banker may be turned off. On the other hand, a banker is likely to be quite interested in seeing a contingency plan that will let you pay back the loan even in the event of a worst-case scenario. The things a banker will look for you to address are:

> ▷ *Cash flow.* One of the most convincing things you can show a banker is the existence of a strong, well-documented flow of cash that will be more than adequate to repay a loan's scheduled principal and interest. Basically, you're going to have to show where you're going to get the money to pay back what you're borrowing.
>
> You'll need more than a projection of future cash flow, by the way. Most bankers will want to see cash flow statements as well as balance sheets and income statements for the past three or so years. And don't forget your tax returns for the same period.

》 *Collateral.* If you're just starting out in business or if you're dealing with a banker who you don't know well, you're unlikely to be able to borrow from a bank without collateral. (That's doubly true if, as is the case with many entrepreneurs, both descriptions apply to you.) Collateral is just something the banker can seize and sell to get back some or all of the money you've borrowed in the event that everything goes wrong and you can't pay it back with profits from operations. It may consist of machinery, equipment, inventory, or all too often, the equity you own in your home. It's advisable NOT to put your home up for collateral—it's simply too big a risk.

But it's a good idea to take the initiative here and propose something that will be used if you suspect a banker will require it. Often the collateral will consist of whatever you're borrowing money to buy—production equipment, computers, a building, and so on.

Why do bankers seek collateral? They have no desire to own secondhand equipment or your house. Experience has taught them that entrepreneurs who have their own assets at risk are more likely to stick to a business than those who have none of their own assets at risk.

---

### 》》 buzzword

A balloon payment is a single, usually final, payment on a loan that is much greater than the payments preceding it. Some business loans, for example, require interest-only payments the first year or two, followed by a single large payment that repays all the principal.

---

》 *Cosigners.* They provide an added layer of protection for lenders. If your own capacity for taking on additional debt is shaky, a cosigner (who is essentially lending you his or her creditworthiness) may make the difference.

》 *Marketing plans.* More than ever before, bankers are taking a closer look at the marketing plans embedded in business plans. Strong competitors, price wars, me-too products, the fickle habits of the buying public, and other market-related risks must be addressed. There are also very web-savvy marketers out there, and it helps if you are tapped into online marketing, such as social media.

Your banker (and most other investors) has to know that you recognize these risks and have well-thought-out ways to deal with them. Besides, it's the cash flow from operations that pays off bank loans.

» *Management.* Bankers like to stress the personal aspect of their services. Many state that they are interested in making loans based on a borrower's character as well as her financial strength. In fact, the borrower's track record and management ability are concerns for bankers evaluating a loan application. If you can show you've run one or more other companies successfully, it will increase your chances of landing a loan to get a startup going.

---

### ⫸ plan pitfall

It seems sensible to plan to put up as collateral the exact item you're borrowing money to buy. But bankers often demand more because it may be impossible to sell the item that you're buying for what you'll owe on it. So, plan to use purchased equipment for part of your collateral but be ready to offer more.

---

### Getting Your House in Order

As an entrepreneur seeking a bank loan, or any type of funding for that matter, you'll want to make sure you have everything in place, including all of your financial documentation as well as your credit history. And if you need to improve your credit history and rating, you should do so in advance. Even if you have previous experience running a business, you'll need to get your personal credit information in order. Start by contacting one of the three major credit bureaus:

» Equifax: 1-800-685-1111, PO Box 740241, Atlanta, GA 30374, www.equifax.com

⟩ Experian: 1-888-397-3742, PO Box 2104, Allen, TX 75013, www.experian.com

⟩ TransUnion: 1-800-916-8800, PO Box 1000, Chester, PA 19016-2000, www.transunion.com

Do this once because loan officers will also inquire, and the more your credit ratings are checked, the more suspicious it may appear to lenders. Also, read your credit reports over *very carefully*, especially if your rating is not as good as you expected it to be. Credit bureaus make more mistakes than you would ever imagine. Make sure there are no errors on your credit reports. If there are errors, call the credit bureau to have them corrected.

### ⟩⟩⟩ fact or fiction

One, two, three strikes you're out. Most small business owners give up after trying three banks. You should be more persistent. Those entrepreneurs that have persisted have found that the fifth, tenth, or even twentieth banker has been impressed enough to give them a loan. Of course, tweaking the business plan based on criticism you receive can, and often does, help improve your odds as you continue going from bank to bank. Listen and learn from feedback and criticism, make changes if you feel the comments are relevant, and keep on going. Be persistent.

### When Bank Financing Is Appropriate

Bank financing is most appropriate for up-and-running enterprises that can show adequate cash flow and collateral to service and secure the loan. Bankers are less likely to provide startup money to turn a concept into a business, and they are even less likely to put up seed money to prove a concept unless you have a track record of launching previous businesses with successful results. Even then, each concept will stand on its own merits.

Bankers are sensitive to the term or length of a loan. Most bank loans are short to intermediate term, meaning they are due in anywhere from less than a year to five years. A short-term loan may be for ninety days and used to finance receivables so you can get a big order out the door. A longer-term loan, up to twenty years, may be used to purchase a piece of long-lasting capital equipment.

## Borrowing When You Really Need It

The old saying about bankers lending only to people who don't need to borrow is almost true. Bankers prefer to lend to companies that are almost, but not quite, financially robust enough to pursue their objective without the loan. Bankers are lenders, not investors. Unlike a venture capitalist who takes an equity position, bankers don't get a higher return on their loan if you happen to be more successful than expected. Their natural tendency is to be conservative.

This is important to understand because it affects how and when you will borrow. You should try to foresee times you'll need to borrow money and arrange a line of credit or other loan before you need it. That will make it easier and, in many cases, cheaper in terms of interest rates than if you wait until you're a needier and, in bankers' eyes, less attractive borrower.

## Credit Unions

Another option when seeking funding is to join a credit union. According to the National Credit Union Administration, there are more than 4,900 credit unions in the country with 131 million members as of March 31, 2022. Because credit unions are not-for-profit financial institutions, their focus is serving the financial needs of their members and not on making a profit. As a result, once you have applied and joined a credit union, it may be easier to get a lower interest rate with fewer fees than can be found at a bank when procuring a loan. However, like a bank, you will still need to prove your creditworthiness and that you can repay the loan or have someone cosign for it.

Because banks have gotten a lot of bad press in recent years for attaching fees to all sorts of activities, many people have switched over to credit unions. One reason is that credit unions typically offer more personalized service, which can include helping you get your house in order before applying for a loan. Credit unions may also offer a sense of camaraderie because they are typically sponsored by a business, a community, or some group of people of which you are one. This can be advantageous because you may find other people interested in your business ideas.

While credit unions are not protected like banks by the FDIC, they are covered by the National Credit Union Share Insurance Fund (NCUSIF). This fund provides federal and most state-chartered credit union members with up to $250,000 of insurance per individual depositor, per federally insured credit union.

## Small Business Administration and Other Government Agencies

Sometimes the government really does want to help. The Small Business Administration (SBA) is devoted to helping small business people get started and run successful businesses. One of its most valuable offerings is a set of financial assistance programs that aim to help you raise the money you need to get started and keep going.

The most popular of several SBA loan programs is the 7(a) General Small Business Loans. The maximum loan amount is $5 million, but as of 2020, the average loan was $567,599. Loans guaranteed by the SBA are assessed a guaranty fee. This fee is based on the loan's maturity and the dollar amount guaranteed, not the total loan amount. The lender initially pays the guaranty fee, and it has the option to pass that expense on to the borrower at closing. The funds to reimburse the lender can be included in the overall loan proceeds.

The SBA website provides a very comprehensive overview of all its loan programs and provides answers to many typical questions. Along with standard business loans, you'll find disaster loans, microloan programs, and real estate and equipment loans.

The SBA can also provide some guarantees. The 7(a) loans, for example, are backed by the full faith and credit of the U.S. government, which guarantees a lender will get back most—but not all—of the money lent out, even if the borrower can't pay. A typical loan guarantee covers 80 percent of the loan. You will find it easier to borrow money and usually get a lower finance rate if you can get an SBA guarantee.

While the SBA sometimes lends money directly to small businesses, most of its financing help is in the form of loan guarantees. To avail yourself of these programs, you need to meet the SBA's definition of a small business and put up pretty much all the business's assets as collateral. Most banks handle SBA-backed loans and can tell you more about the programs. It's easier to learn by going to the SBA.gov website and reviewing its loans. You can also visit one of the SBA district offices.

---

### ⟫ plan pointer

Lenders look for borrowers exhibiting the four Cs of credit:

1. *Character.* What's your reputation and record?
2. *Capacity or cash flow.* Do you have sufficient cash flow to repay principal and interest?
3. *Capital.* Does your business have enough capital to keep going if you can't pay the debt from earnings?
4. *Collateral.* Do you own something valuable the banker can take if you can't pay the loan back?

---

## Angel Investors

If you are having trouble getting funding for your venture under the right terms, or under any terms at all, you'll be glad to know about the existence of angels in the investment world. Angels are individuals who invest their own money, as opposed to institutions or professional money managers, who invest other people's money. Many angels are well-off professionals, such as doctors and lawyers. Some are retired but have tremendous expertise to share in a specific field. Others are successful small business owners who have made a bundle with their own entrepreneurial efforts and are now interested in letting their money work for them in someone else's venture.

### Finding an Angel

Angel investors used to be a difficult group to find. Not so any longer. There are groups formed by angels and other organizations, such as Funding Post (fundingpost.com), that

WRITE Your Business Plan  ▷  71

arrange for special angel and venture capitalist showcases in various parts of the country. You can sign up and pay to attend an event at which up-and-coming entrepreneurs, like yourself, get to meet with many angel investors and VCs in one place. Have your short elevator pitch (discussed at the end of the book) ready and demonstrate the enthusiasm you have for your new business.

Because angels invest their own money, you might think they are the most discriminating, difficult-to-please investors. In fact, they are as a rule much more willing to take a flier on a risky, unproven idea than are professional investors and lenders.

Angels often take a personal interest in a project and may simply believe strongly in the person behind it . . . that's you! They are usually swayed more by personal concerns than by financial ones.

While angel investors used to be located primarily by word of mouth, they are easier to find in the electronic age. The Angel Investment Network helps angel investors and small businesses seeking capital meet online. To learn more, visit www.angelinvestmentnetwork.us.

---

### ⟫⟫ buzzword

Due diligence refers to all the things an investor should do to check out an investment. It has a legal definition when applied to the responsibilities of financial professionals, such as stockbrokers. In general, it includes such things as requiring audited financial statements and checking warehouses for claimed inventory stocks.

---

The Angel Capital Association is another place to learn about angels and seek out an angel network—a local group of angel investors in your area. Visit them at www.angelcapitalassociation.org. They can also be reached at (913) 894-4700.

Chapter 4 / Digging for Dollars

Keep in mind that angels are, above all else, unconventional. Many have little training in evaluating business ideas. If twenty angels turn you down, it doesn't mean a thing. Until you've gone through the last name in your Rolodex, you still have a chance of landing an angel backer.

Consider Harold Lacy's "six degrees of separation" method. Your angel might be somebody you know, recommended by somebody you know, or a local investment club, business person, perhaps even a local development agency.

Angel investors often focus on local markets, specific industries, and affinities such as college or university alumni. Your search should include looking for angel groups related to the college or university from which you graduated; your town, or state; and the industry you're in.

Use web search. Search for "angel investors in [your area]" or "angel investors [your type of business]" or "angel investors [your college or university] alumni."

(Tim Berry, "How to Write a Convincing Business Plan for InvestorsHow to Land Funding From Angel Investors", Bplans, https://articles.bplans.com/securing-angel-investors/, 7/29/19)

### Small Business Investment Company Program

The SBA has a program that bridges the capital gap between loans (direct or guaranteed) and equity investments, which are the most difficult to find. Most banks are unwilling to offer very long-term loans (sometimes called "quasi-capital"), and most venture capital firms are unwilling to invest under $3 million in businesses that are unlikely to go public or be acquired for a fancy multiple within three to five years. Enter the Small Business Investment Company (SBIC).

Congress created the SBIC program in 1958 to fill the gap between the availability of venture capital and the needs of small businesses in startup and growth situations. SBICs, licensed and regulated by the SBA, are privately owned and managed investment firms that use their own capital plus funds borrowed at favorable rates with an SBA guarantee to make venture capital investments in small businesses.

Virtually all SBICs are profit-motivated businesses. They provide equity capital, long-term loans, debt equity investments, and management assistance to qualifying small businesses. Their incentive is the chance to share in the success of the small business as it grows and prospers.

There are two types of SBICs: regular SBICs and specialized SBICs, also known as 301(d) SBICs. Specialized SBICs invest in small businesses owned by entrepreneurs who are socially or economically disadvantaged, mainly members of minority groups.

The program makes funding available to all types of manufacturing and service industries. Many investment companies seek out small businesses with new products or services because of the strong growth potential of such firms. Some SBICs specialize in the field in which their management has special knowledge or competency. Most, however, consider a wide variety of investment opportunities. Go to www.sba.gov/partners/sbics for a listing of SBICs.

You may also fit angel guidelines if you don't need a whole lot of money. Institutional venture capitalists can, by pooling the funds of several different groups, raise vast sums. It's not unheard of for venture capitalists to invest nine-figure sums—more than $100 million—in relatively new, unproven ventures. Even Bill Gates or Warren Buffett is unlikely to feel comfortable sinking that kind of money into anything uncertain. Your angels' capacity will vary, of course, but angels tend to start small and see how you are doing before adding to the pot. One of the nicest things about the angel networks that have formed in recent years is that they can pool their resources, giving you a few angel investors in one place at one time. This also makes it easier when you are preparing to meet with angel investors. Rather than meeting one at a time, you can meet several in one angel network or even a couple who will spread the word among their partners so that they can decide as a group.

---

### ⟫⟫ plan pointer

If you're after angels, it's in your interest to guard their interests. Unsophisticated angels may, for instance, give you money without specifying exactly what they are buying, such as percentage of ownership. Such angels can be taken advantage of. But you may want more help someday, and angels tend to talk with each other. So make it legal, make terms clear, and take care of their interests.

---

## Venture Capitalists

Venture capitalists represent the most glamorous and appealing form of financing to many entrepreneurs. They are known for backing high-risk companies in the early stages, and a lot of the best-known entrepreneurial success stories owe their early financing to venture capitalists.

When many entrepreneurs write a business plan, obtaining venture capital backing is what they have in mind. That's understandable. Venture capitalists are associated with business success. They can provide large sums of money, valuable advice, priceless contacts, and considerable prestige by their mere presence. Just the fact that you've obtained venture capital backing means your business has, in their eyes at least, considerable potential for rapid and profitable growth.

Venture capitalists both lend to and make equity investments in young companies. The loans are often expensive, carrying rates of up to 20 percent. They sometimes also provide what may seem like very cheap capital. That means you don't have to pay out hard-to-get cash in the form of interest and principal installments. Instead, you give a portion of your or other owners' interest in the company in exchange for the VC's backing.

### When Venture Capital Is an Option

Venture capital is most often used to finance companies that are young without being babies and that are established without being mature. But it can also help struggling firms as well as those that are on the edge of breaking into the big time.

The following are the major types and sources of capital, along with distinguishing characteristics of each.

- *Seed money.* Seed money is the initial capital required to transform a business from an idea into an enterprise. Venture capitalists are not as likely to provide seed money as some other, less tough-minded financing sources, such as family investors. However, venture capitalists will back seedlings if the idea is strong enough and the prospects promising enough. If they see something new and exciting (usually an aspect of technology) and foresee rapid growth (and a strong potential for high earnings), they may jump in and back a fledgling startup. It's a long shot, but it does happen.

  VCs, however, are less likely to provide equity capital to a seed-money-stage entrepreneur than they are to provide debt financing. This may come in the form of a straight loan, usually some kind of subordinated debt. It may also involve a purchase of bonds issued by the company. Frequently these will be convertible bonds that can be exchanged for shares of stock. Venture capitalists may also purchase shares of preferred stock in a startup. Holders of preferred shares receive dividends before common stockholders and also get paid before other shareholders if the company is dissolved.

  Seed money is usually a relatively small amount of cash, up to $250,000 or so, that is used to prove a business concept has merit. It may be earmarked for producing working prototypes, doing market research, or otherwise testing the waters before committing to a full-scale endeavor.

- *Startup capital.* Startup capital is financing used to get a business with a proven idea up and running. For example, a manufacturer might use startup capital to get production underway, set up marketing, and create some actual sales. This amount may reach $1 million.

  Venture capitalists frequently are enthusiastic financiers of startups because they carry less risk than companies at the seed money stage but still offer the prospect of the high return on investment that VCs require.

- *Later-round financing.* Venture capitalists may also come in on some later rounds of financing. First-stage financing is usually used to set up full-scale production and market development. Second-stage financing is used to expand the operations of an already up-and-running enterprise, often through financing receivables, adding production capacity, or boosting marketing. Mezzanine financing, an even later stage, may be required for a major expansion of profitable and robust enterprises. Bridge financing is often the last stage before a company goes public. It may be used to sustain a growing company during the often lengthy process of preparing and completing a public offering of stock.

  Venture capitalists even invest in companies that are in trouble. These turnaround investments can be riskier than startups and therefore even more expensive to the entrepreneurs involved.

Venture capital isn't for everybody, but it provides a very important financing option for some young firms. When you're writing a business plan to raise money, you may want to consider venture capitalists and their unique needs.

## What Venture Capitalists Want

While venture capitalists come in many forms, they have similar goals. They want their money back, and they want it back with a lot of interest and capital growth.

VCs typically invest in companies that they foresee being sold either to the public or to larger firms within the next several years. As part owners of the firm, they'll get their rewards when such sales go through. Of course, if there's no sale or if the company goes bankrupt, they don't even get their initial money back.

---

⟩⟩ **plan pitfall**

Many VCs insist on placing one or more directors on the boards of companies they finance. And these directors are rarely there just to observe. They take an active role in running the company.

VCs also are reluctant to provide financing without obtaining an interest in the companies they back, sometimes a very significant and controlling interest. This can make them just as influential as if they had a majority of the directors on the board, or more so.

---

VCs aren't quite the plungers they may seem. They're willing to assume risk, but they want to minimize it as much as possible. Therefore, they typically look for certain features in companies they are going to invest in. Those include:

⟩ Rapid sales growth
⟩ A proprietary new technology or dominant position in an emerging market
⟩ A sound management team
⟩ The potential to be acquired by a larger company or be taken public in a stock offering within three to five years
⟩ High rates of return on their investment

## Rates of Return

Like most financiers, venture capitalists want the return of any funds they lend or use to purchase equity interest in companies. But VCs have some very special requirements when it comes to the terms they want and, especially, the rates of return they demand.

Venture capitalists require that their investments have the likelihood of generating very high rates of return. A 30 percent to 50 percent annual rate of return is a benchmark many venture capitalists seek. That means if a venture capitalist invested $1 million in your firm and expected to sell out in three years with a 35 percent annual gain, he or she would have to be able to sell the stake for approximately $2.5 million.

These are high rates of return compared with the 2.5 percent or so usually offered by ten-year U.S. Treasury notes and the nearly 10 percent historical return of the U.S. stock market. Venture capitalists justify their desires for such high rates of return by the fact that their investments are high-risk.

Most venture-backed companies, in fact, are not successful and generate losses for their investors. Venture capitalists hedge their bets by taking a portfolio approach: If one in ten of their investments takes off and six do OK, then the three that stumble or fail will be a minor nuisance rather than an economic cold bath.

## Cashing-Out Options

One key concern of venture capitalists is a way to cash out their investment. This is typically done through a sale of all or part of the company, either to a larger firm through an acquisition or to the public through an initial offering of stock.

In effect, this need for cashing-out options means that if your company isn't seen as a likely candidate for a buyout or an initial public offering (IPO) in the next five years or so, VCs aren't going to be interested.

---

### ⟫ buzzword

Rate of return is the income or profit earned by an investor on capital invested in a company. It is usually expressed as an annual percentage.

---

## Being Acquired

A common way for venture capitalists to cash out is for the company to be acquired, usually by a larger firm. An acquisition can occur through a merger or by means of a payment of cash, stock, debt, or some combination.

Mergers and acquisitions don't have to meet the strict regulatory requirements of public stock offerings, so they can be completed much more quickly, easily, and cheaply than an IPO. Buyers will want to see audited financials, but you—or the financiers who may wind up controlling your company—can literally strike a deal to sell the company over lunch or a game of golf. About the only roadblocks that could be thrown up would be if you couldn't finalize the terms of the deal, if it turned out that your company wasn't what it seemed, or, rarely, if the buyout resulted in a monopoly that generated resistance from regulators.

Venture capitalists assessing your firm's acquisition chances are going to look for characteristics like proprietary technology, distribution systems, or product lines that other companies might want to possess. They also like to see larger, preferably acquisition-minded, firms in your industry. For instance, Microsoft, the world's largest software firm, frequently acquires small personal computer software firms with talented personnel or unique technology. Venture capitalists looking at funding a software company are almost certain to include an assessment of whether Microsoft might be interested in buying out the company someday.

---

⟫⟫ **plan pitfall**

Some VCs specialize in a field, such as retail, biotechnology, or high tech. Others have a regional focus. But whatever his or her special interests, almost any venture capitalist will admit to desiring the basic characteristics of steady growth, market dominance, sound management, and potential for going public in an investment.

---

## Going Public: Initial Public Offerings (IPOs)

Some fantastic fortunes have been created in recent years by venture-funded startups that went public. Initial public offerings of their stock have made numerous millionaires, seemingly overnight. For example, when Twitter made its initial public offering at a price of $26 in November 2013, the stock took off, gaining as much as 93 percent within a day and creating 1,600 millionaires. Wow! IPOs have made many millions for the venture investors who provided early stage financing.

The 2012 passage of the Jumpstart Our Small Business Startups (JOBS) Act allows for confidential filing of IPO-related documents. This has made it easier for small business owners who do not want their numbers getting out to the public too soon. There was often concern about investors getting too much preliminary information that could influence their decision to commit to the company. Confidentiality has increased the number of IPO filings in the small business community.

Nonetheless, an IPO takes lots of time. You'll need to add outside directors to your board and clean up the terms of any sweetheart deals with managers, family, or board members as well as have a major accounting firm audit your operations for several years before going public. If you need money today, in other words, an IPO isn't going to provide it.

An IPO is also probably the most expensive way to raise money in terms of the amount you have to lay out up front. The bills for accountants, lawyers, printing, and miscellaneous fees for even a modest IPO will easily reach six figures. For this reason, IPOs are best used to raise amounts at least equal to millions of dollars in equity capital. Venture capitalists keep all these requirements in mind when assessing an investment's potential for going public. Keep in mind that the number of new businesses that go public is quite small.

### ⟫⟫ plan of action

The National Association of Certified Valuation Analysts is the trade group for people whose business is deciding what businesses are worth. It can help you find a valuation analyst as well as learn the basics of figuring a business's worth. Contact NACVA at NACVA.com or call them at (800) 677-2009.

## Bonds

There are two kinds of debt financing: straight loans and bonds. Bonds give you a way to borrow from a number of people without having to do separate deals with each of them. If you need to borrow $500,000, for instance, you can issue 500 bonds in $1,000 denominations. Then you can sell those bonds to anyone who'll buy them, including family, friends, venture capitalists, and other investors subject to stringent legal constraints.

Corporations use a bewildering variety of bonds for financing, but the most common type simply calls for you to pay a stated amount of interest on the face amount for a certain period. After that time, usually five years, you pay back the face amount to the buyer.

Bonds give you the great advantage of being able to set the interest rate and terms and amount you're trying to raise instead of having to take whatever a lender offers. The problem with bonds is that they are regulated similarly to public stock offerings. So, although they're widely used by big companies, very few small companies issue them.

There is an exception to this general rule. Some states pool together long-term loans in state-guaranteed industrial bonds for industrial (read: job-creating) businesses. This has the advantage of lowering the issuing costs for the companies involved while providing the patient quasi-capital they need to succeed. Check with your state's economic development department.

---

⟫⟫ **fact or fiction**

Many entrepreneurs dream of going public. But IPOs are not for every firm. The ideal IPO candidate has a record of rapidly growing sales and earnings and operates in a high-profile industry. Some have a lot of one and not much of the other. Low earnings but lots of interest characterize many biotech and internet-related IPOs. These tech companies are usually the ones that generate the huge IPOs and instant millionaires we read about.

---

## Indirect Funding Sources

Direct funding sources put money into your business. Indirect funding sources postpone taking money out of the business, thus conserving working capital. Trade credit is far and away the most important indirect source of funding.

### Trade Credit

You don't need a loan application, permission from the Securities and Exchange Commission, or even a note from your mother to take advantage of one of the most useful and popular forms of financing around. Trade credit, the credit extended to you by suppliers who let you buy now and pay later, can make a substantial difference to your cash flow.

You can measure the amount of trade credit you have outstanding by simply adding up all your accounts payable, or the amount outstanding of bills on your desk. Any time you take delivery of materials, equipment, or other valuables without paying cash on the spot, you're using trade credit.

For many businesses, trade credit is an essential form of financing. For instance, the owner of a clothing store who receives a shipment of bathing suits in April may not have to pay for them until June. By that time, she can hope to have sold enough of the suits to pay for the shipment. Without the trade credit, she'd have to look to a bank or another source for financing.

### Factoring

Factoring is the flip side of trade credit. It's what happens when a supplier sells its accounts receivables to a financial specialist, called a factor. The factor immediately pays the amount of the receivables, less a discount, and receives the payments when they arrive from customers. Factoring is an important form of finance in many industries.

## Chapter 5 Summary

The process of writing your business plan helps you take a thorough, careful, and comprehensive look at the most important facets of your business, including the contexts in which it operates. Just raising questions can sometimes lead to a solution, or at least ensure that if conditions change you won't be forced to make decisions hastily. The ongoing "what if this or that happens?" inherent in the planning process keeps you alert. In other words, the planning process itself makes you a far more capable manager and entrepreneur than you would be without it. For many, this is a more valuable result than securing funding.

In many ways, writing a business plan is an end in itself. The process will teach you a lot about your business that you are unlikely to learn by any other process. You'll spot future trouble areas, identify opportunities, build confidence in the strength of your ideas, and help your organization run smoothly, simply through the act of writing a plan.

What you'll learn from this chapter:

- How to properly evaluate a new venture
- Why you should use your business plan to inform suppliers and customers
- How to manage with your plan
- How to monitor the performance of your business
- How to use your plan to attract good people
- Why you should always update your plan

# Put Your
# Plan to Work

## Evaluating a New Venture

Numbers can lie, of course, and nobody can create a spreadsheet that really tells the future. But evaluating financial data is to entrepreneurship what evaluating lab results is to a medical doctor. If your vital signs are good, odds are your future will be as well.

But what if the odds don't look so favorable? What if the first pass through your cash flow projection or income pro formas contains more red than a fire station paint locker? Sure, you can go back and look for an error or an overly pessimistic or conservative assumption. You can even try altering a few of the inevitable numbers that you really have no way of estimating accurately to see where the pressure points are, if nothing else.

But what if you do that, even pushing your alterations past the point of credibility, and your plan still doesn't make sense? Well, in that case, you've probably done yourself the really big favor of finding out something isn't going to work before you sink your money into it. Nobody knows exactly how often this happens, but it's safe to say that a lot of businesses are never attempted because the plan convincingly says that they shouldn't be.

Is that bad? Well, it may feel bad. But think how much worse you would feel if you went ahead with the venture, and things turned out as the plan forecast. Business planning is a powerful tool for evaluating the feasibility of business ventures. Use it.

It would be a shame to keep the benefits of a well-done plan to yourself. And you shouldn't. You can use your plan to find funding. But a good plan can also help sell your products, services, and your whole company to prospects and suppliers. Furthermore, a plan is a valuable tool for communicating your visions, goals, and objectives to other managers and key employees in your firm.

## Informing Suppliers and Customers

Increasingly, companies large and small have been trying to trim the number of suppliers and customers they deal with and develop deeper and stronger relationships with the ones they keep. An essential part of this is getting to know more about existing and prospective vendors and clients. So don't be surprised if one day, when you're trying to set up a new supplier relationship or pitch a deal to a big company, the person you're negotiating with asks to see your business plan.

Why do suppliers care about business plans? Suppliers want to sell only to people who can pay, which is one important reason a new supplier could ask to see your business plan before taking a big order. Remember, if a supplier is selling to you on credit—letting you take delivery of goods and pay for them later—that supplier is, in effect, your lender. Suppliers who sell for other than cash on delivery have the same legitimate interest in your business's strategy and soundness as does a banker.

Say a supplier's analysis of customer records shows it has a knack for developing long-term profitable relationships with moderate-sized companies that emphasize excellent service, price at a premium level, and provide only the best merchandise. Business plans provide all the information such a company will need to find and clone its best customers. So if a supplier asks to see your plan, be willing to share it. It could be the start of a long and mutually beneficial relationship.

Customers are likely to be concerned about how well your respective strategies fit with theirs. For instance, say your mission statement says that you intend to produce the best-in-the-world example of your product no matter what the cost. Your customer, meanwhile, is a high-volume, low-price reseller of the type of products you make. Even if your offering fits the customer's need this time, odds are good that the relationship won't work out over the long haul. If, on the other hand, a look at your business plan reveals that your companies share the same kind of strategies and have similar objectives in type if not scope, it's an encouraging sign.

⟫⟫⟫ **plan pointer**

A confidentiality statement helps control the spread of proprietary information. It should say something like: "The attached document contains privileged information. Please do not show it to anybody else or discuss the contents." You then have the other party sign it and date it. Get your attorney to help with the wording or visit Nolo.com where you can find samples.

## Managing with Your Plan

The spread of the open-book management theory means a lot more employees are seeing their companies' business plans than ever before. When employees get the key information managers are using to make decisions, they understand management better and make better decisions themselves, and efficiency and profitability often increase as a result. This is transparency in business.

Many companies hold annual meetings at which they present an edited version of the business plan and discuss it with their employees. You can also use bulletin boards or company newsletters to publish smaller sections of your plan, such as your mission statement or some details of financial objectives and how you're progressing.

One drawback to using excerpts of a business plan to help inform and manage your employees is that some people won't understand it, especially taken out of context. Often, companies have some materials to email employees about reading financial reports, as well as other topics.

"We've found one meeting that is simply indispensable. It only takes an hour each month, keeps the management team up to speed on everything that's going on in the company, and helps us plan and manage in a quick and effective way.

This meeting is our monthly plan review meeting. It's a time for you and your team to review current progress against your ideal performance. This one-to-two-hour meeting should be spent dissecting parts of your strategy, reviewing financials, and making adjustments based on overall performance.

Every business of any size can benefit from a calculated time to stop, review and revise. When done correctly, this meeting can help you focus on what's vital for your company, identify what data you need to accurately measure it and how to best present and review these results."

(Noah Parsons, "How to Conduct a Monthly Business Plan Review Meeting", LivePlan, https://www.liveplan.com/blog/how-to-run-a-monthly-plan-review-meeting/, 6/21/21)

## Monitoring the Performance of Your Business

Using a business plan to monitor your performance has many benefits. If your cash flow is running much shorter than projected at the moment, even though you're not currently in trouble, that information may help you to spot disaster before it occurs. By comparing plan projections with actual results, you gain a deeper understanding of your business's pressure points or the components of your operation that have the most effect on results.

## Spotting Trouble Early

You don't have to be a wizard to get some solid hints about the future beyond tomorrow, especially when it comes to the operations of your own business. You can look at virtually any page of your business plan and find an important concept or number describing some expected future event that, if it turns out to be diverging from reality, may hint at future trouble.

Say your profit margins are shrinking slowly but steadily, and the trend seems irreversible. If you notice that within a few months your declining margins will push your break-even point too high to live with, you can act now to fix the problem. You may need to add a new, higher-margin product, get rid of an old one, or begin stressing marketing to a more profitable clientele. All these moves, and many more you could take, have a good chance of working if your careful comparison of plan projections with actual results warns you of impending danger. Use the projections in your business plan as guideposts as you move forward.

> "When you review your actual results against your plan, look for problems and opportunities. If sales aren't meeting expectations, think about your marketing and sales strategies and if you should refine those. Maybe you should adjust your spending and refine your expense budget moving forward.
>
> On the other hand, maybe part of your business is doing better than expected. You might want to consider focusing more on that part of the business or using excess revenue in one area to fund development or marketing in another area."
>
> (Noah Parsons, "Growth Planning — The Modern Way to Write a Business Plan", LivePlan, https://www.liveplan.com/blog/growth-planning-process-explained/, 11/15/22)

### Understanding Pressure Points

Not all tips that come from comparing plans with results have to do with avoiding danger. Some help you to identify profit opportunities. Others may show how seemingly minor tweaks can produce outsized improvements in sales or profitability. For example, the plan for a one-person professional service business indicated that rising sales were not, in general, accompanied by rising costs. Fixed items such as office rent and insurance stayed the same, and even semivariable costs such as electric bills will vary only slightly. The bulk of any extra business went straight to the bottom line, showing up as profit improvement. But one cost that didn't seem especially variable went up sharply as business volume climbed. That was the number of transactions.

Ordinarily this would be a given and not necessarily a matter of grave concern. A large enterprise would simply hire a few more modestly paid customer service reps, credit department staff members, or bookkeepers to handle the added orders, invoices, and the like. For this single professional, however, added paperwork comes at a very high cost—her own time.

Somehow in her projections of steadily rising sales volume, she had neglected to note that more business meant more invoices to be sent out, more account statements to be mailed or emailed, more customers to be reminded to pay, more time spent on banking needs, and so on. All this work, while not necessarily unpleasant, was taking up more and more of her time.

As a part of checking her plan against results, she noticed this unexpected increase in transactions and figured out what it meant. She calculated that, when taking all paperwork into account, she spent roughly an hour on each transaction no matter how large or small. She realized that one of the most important pressure points in her business was related to the size of a transaction. By refusing small engagements and seeking clients who could offer big jobs, she would reduce the amount of time spent on otherwise unproductive paperwork and increase the time she could spend completing client requirements.

Ultimately, she was able to trim what had been 100 annual transactions down to seventy-five, while increasing the amount of her dollar revenue. The result was a free twenty-five hours to spend working on more business or even vacationing. If you can see and relieve a pressure point like that, you can really keep your business from boiling over.

There are few things to equal the sensation of filling in all the numbers on a cash flow projection, hitting the recalculate button, and scrolling to the bottom of your spreadsheet to see what the future holds. If the news is good and you see a steady string of positive cash balances across the bottom row, you know that, assuming your data is good and your assumptions reasonable, your business has a good chance of making it.

> "Don't beat yourself up if you aren't meeting or beating your plan. The goal of tracking your performance is not to "stay on plan" but to make adjustments if things aren't going "to" plan."
>
> (Noah Parsons, "Growth Planning — The Modern Way to Write a Business Plan", LivePlan, https://www.liveplan.com/blog/growth-planning-process-explained/, 11/15/22)

### ≫≫ plan pitfall

The fact that your business is unlikely to perform exactly as planned is no reason to skip planning! A plan isn't worthless just because it doesn't present the future with perfect accuracy. At worst it can help you monitor how reality is stacking up to your plan. If your plan seems way off base, you may need a fix—or another plan.

## Do the Numbers Add Up?

Many businesses fail because of events that are impossible to foresee. If you'd begun a car dealership specializing in yacht-sized gas guzzlers right before the Arab oil embargo in the 1970s, you would probably have been out of business in less time than one had to sit on the resulting lines at gas stations, through no fault of your own. The same might go for a software startup that comes out with a new program just before Google unveils a top-secret, long-term development effort to create something that does the same job for a lot less money.

It's probably not a bad idea, as part of your business planning process, to include some information in your business plan about the activities or intentions of potential embargoes. If nothing else, crafting a backup plan is a good idea should something happen that is out of your control. Preparation for unexpected disasters can make or break your business. The companies that had off-site backup of their documents after Hurricane Katrina hit New Orleans in 2005 had far better chances of restarting their businesses than those that had to begin from scratch. Of course, some things are just wild cards and can't be predicted. For these you just have to trust the luck of the draw.

So, what numbers have to add up? Certainly, you have to be selling your products and services at a profit that will let you sustain the business long term. You'll also have to have a financial structure, including payables-and-receivables systems and financing, that will keep you from running out of cash even once. If you have investors who want to sell the company someday, you may need a plan with a big number in the field for shareholders' equity on the projected balance sheet.

"It's important to review your cash position and cash flow. From an accounting standpoint, your business may look profitable. However, without knowing how much cash you have on hand, tracking outstanding expenses, and other risk factors, that profitability can quickly disappear. That's why reviewing your cash flow statement is so crucial, as it's meant to help you understand the health of your business."

(Noah Parsons, "Cash Flow Analysis Explained — How to Review Your Cash Flow Statement", LivePlan, https://www.liveplan.com/blog/cash-flow-analysis/, 7/7/21)

>>> **plan of action**

While putting together your numbers, include a capital reserve fund to spend on special projects or to be used for unforeseen emergencies.

When you're asking yourself whether the numbers add up, keep the needs of your business and your business partners in mind. Even if it looks like it'll take an air strike to keep your business from getting started, you don't want to do it if the numbers say that, long term, it's headed nowhere. Therefore, you need to look carefully at the trends in your industry and try to determine where it will be in five, ten, or twenty years. No, it's not easy to do, but you can see where innovation and new ideas are coming from and how they might change the face of your industry.

>>> **plan of action**

The Employee Benefit Research Institute (EBRI) conducts regular studies and surveys to find out what employees want and what employers are giving them. To learn more about what benefits you should offer to attract the best, go to EBRI.org or call them at (202) 659-0670.

## Attracting Good People

"Good people" is a very subjective term. A person with a great resume, treated poorly by management, is no longer very motivated and likely NOT to be a "good person." Conversely a "bad person," based on what you have on paper, may, with some training, trust, and fair treatment, turn out to be a very good hire.

Nonetheless, a good business plan can help you attract what are considered to be "good people," from managers and other employees to vendors, suppliers, and partners. It gives people the idea that you have a well-thought-out plan of action so they have more confidence that you have credibility and feel they are not jumping on board what may soon be a sinking ship. It can also give up-and-comers the idea that you offer training and advancement.

What you offer as an entrepreneur will determine whom you will attract. In any economy, good or bad, people want to be treated with respect and are more likely to become part of your team if they see advancement and a corporate culture they can embrace. Therefore, just like dating, you need to present yourself and your business in a way that will give others a positive impression.

## Prospective Partners

Partners are like any other investor, and it would be a rare one who would come on board without some kind of plan. Partners want to know your basic business concept, the market, and your strategy for attacking it; who else is on your team; what your financial performance, strengths, and needs are; and what's in it for them. Luckily, these are exactly the same questions a business plan is designed to address, so you're likely to please even a demanding prospective partner by simply showing him or her a well-prepared plan. The one difference is a plan probably won't contain the details of a partnership agreement. And you'll need one of these to spell out the conditions of your partnership, no matter how well you and your prospective partner know, understand, and trust one another. Have an attorney who is familiar with partnerships help draft the paperwork so you are on the same page from the start and know exactly what is expected of each partner.

## Take a Conservative Stance

While you don't want to fail, there is a point when writing a business plan that you admit the possibility of failure. It's only natural to create a plan that will describe a roaring success, but you have to be careful not to present an overly optimistic view, especially of such elements as sales, costs, and profit margins.

It's tempting to noodle around with the numbers until you come up with the desired result. And if you make only small changes here and there, it may seem all right. What difference does it make? Say you increase your projected market share by 1 percent here, reduce expected costs by 2 percent there, and lower your estimate of required startup capital by a few percentage points as well.

A number of similarly small changes, in sum, can make a big difference in the bottom line of your plan and turn what otherwise looks like a loser into a projected winner. But don't be seduced. You may be asking for investments from friends and family you care about as well as putting your own life savings into the enterprise. The feelings of arm's-length investors may not be so important, but if you mislead them in your plan, you may open yourself up to accusation of misrepresentation.

Looking at things in your plan through rose-colored glasses may even doom your business to failure if it causes you to seek insufficient startup capital, underprice your product or service, or expect unrealistically rapid growth. Temper your enthusiasm. If your plan indicates that the business idea isn't sound, by all means look for errors. But don't make the mistake of skewing your plan to fit an idea that isn't sound.

CEO Sabrina Parsons of Palo Alto Software (makers of LivePlan), emphasizes the importance of continuously referring back to your business plan no matter the stage of one's business journey—she calls this growth planning. She says, "People always ask me: what is the number one thing they should do to run a better business? And I think the best answer I can give them is to create a growth plan. They don't want a traditional long-form business plan—nobody does that anymore, and you hear that all the time. Whether you're just starting your business or you've been running your business for twenty years, everybody is looking for some type of growth. Your growth may be in opening new locations and actually physically growing the business. The growth might be in revenue, but the growth simply might be how much money you can bring in, where your profits are at, how profitable you are. Or maybe the growth is in being able to afford a manager so that you can actually take a vacation. That's what growth planning is," (Parsons, Sabrina. Interview. Conducted by Makenna Crocker. 30 November 2022).

## Always Update Your Plan

Writing a business plan is one of those skills that improves with practice. The first one or two times you create a plan you may feel a little unsure of yourself and even less certain that what you're doing has value.

If you go on to start several ventures during your career, you'll naturally write several business plans, and each one will be better than the last. It's likely as well that with better planning skills will come improved business skills, boosting the odds that each successive company you start will do better than the previous one.

But there's no reason that only serial entrepreneurs should get the benefit of regular business planning sessions. If you start just one company, or even if you never start a company at all, you should be constantly honing your business planning skills by updating your business plan.

Updating a plan is normally easier than starting from scratch. Instead of trying to figure out what your basic business concept is, you only have to decide whether it's changing. You'll usually be able to reuse the financial formulas, spreadsheets, management biographies, and other more or less evergreen contents of your plan.

### Will You Need to Update Your Plan?

Here are nine reasons to think about updating your plan. If one applies to you, it's time for an update.

1. A new financial period is about to begin. You may update your plan annually, quarterly, or even monthly if your industry changes quickly.
2. You need financing. Lenders and other financiers need an updated plan to make financing decisions.
3. Your customers' needs and desires have changed. Talk to your customers often to find out what they're buying, if your solutions still meet their needs, and if you can provide new solutions for them.

4. Significant markets change. Shifting client tastes, consolidation trends among customers, and altered regulatory climates can trigger a need for plan updates.

5. New or stronger competitors are looking to your customers for their growth.

6. Your firm develops a new product, technology, service, or skill. If your business has changed a lot since you wrote your plan, it's time for an update.

7. You have had a change in management. New managers should get fresh information.

8. Your company has crossed a threshold, such as moving out of your home office, reaching $1 million in sales, or employing 100 people.

9. Your old plan doesn't seem to reflect reality anymore. Maybe you did a poor job last time. Maybe things have just changed faster than you expected. But if your plan seems irrelevant, redo it.

It's important, however, that a plan update not be a mechanical task, limited to plugging in the most recent sales figures. Take the time to challenge some of the core assumptions of your prior plan to see if they still hold up. Have profit margins been higher than you expected? Then start planning how to make the most of any extra cash you generate. Is your new retail store unit not performing as well as others or you expected? Then now's the time to figure out why. Has competition for your new product arisen sooner than you guessed? Take a look at other products with an eye to seeing if they are also more vulnerable than you think.

In large corporations with strict planning routines requiring annual, semiannual, and quarterly plans and plan updates, managers spend at least part of their time working on or thinking about a new plan or plan update. All that information flowing up to senior managers in the form of plans helps keep the brass informed. It helps those in the trenches, too. It's a fact that everybody is judged by past performance. And the best way to ensure that a year from now you'll be looking back on your performance with satisfaction and pride is to plan now and often.

> "Don't feel like it's a requirement to update your plan. You should only refine your plan if your strategy either isn't working OR things are going much better than you had originally planned. If you're meeting your expectations, staying the course might be the best bet."
>
> (Noah Parsons, "Growth Planning — The Modern Way to Write a Business Plan", LivePlan, https://www.liveplan.com/blog/growth-planning-process-explained/, 11/15/22)

# Framing Your Plan

## *Section Summary*

Once you've laid your foundation that you did in Chapters 1 through 5, you need to create a frame for your building in which your business can operate. As with any building, the frame needs to include all the features so you can use the building from day one.

This section begins by discussing the overall view of your plans in your executive summary in Chapter 6. You may need a team of builders, and Chapter 7 explains how to explain your management team to readers. In Chapter 8, you'll learn how to tell people what it is you sell. Next, Chapter 9 talks about how to examine your industry and how your business serves customers within it. Then Chapter 10 tells you how you need to explain to readers how you're going to market your plan to help it grow. Aside from external marketing, Chapter 11 tells you how you'll tell readers how your business works internally. Finally, Chapter 12 talks about how to show people your financial statements and how you forecast revenue will grow.

## Chapter 6 Summary

The first part of your plan that anybody will see, after the title page and table of contents, is the executive summary. This could be considered an expanded table of contents (in prose form) because it's more than an introduction to the rest of the plan. It's supposed to be a brief look at the key elements of the whole plan—and it's critical.

What you'll learn from this chapter:

> How to approach your summary
> The purposes of a summary
> How to communicate your big idea to your readers
> An understanding of how much cash you need and the goals of financiers
> How to tell people who will own what
> How to give your business story a happy ending
> How to provide a company description and any optional information
> How to extract the essence of the plan for your summary

# Executive Summaries Sell Ideas

The actual executive summary should be only a page or two. In it you may include your mission and vision statements, a brief sketch of your plans and goals, a quick look at your company and its organization, an outline of your strategy, and highlights of your financial status and needs. If you've ever read a CliffsNotes version of a classic novel, you get the idea. Your executive summary is the CliffsNotes of your business plan.

Labor over your summary. Polish it. Refine it. Ask friends and colleagues to take a look at it, and then take their suggestions to heart. If your plan isn't getting the response that you want when you put it to work, suspect a flaw in the summary. If you get a chance to look at another plan that was used to raise a pile of cash, give special scrutiny to the executive summary.

The summary is the most important part of your whole plan. Even if a plan is relatively short, it's difficult for most people to keep that much information in their minds at once. It's much easier to get your arms around the amount of information—just one or two pages—in an executive summary. Your plan is going to be judged on what you include in the summary and on how well you present it.

"The executive summary is like an elevator pitch. You're selling someone on reading your full plan while quickly summarizing the key points. Readers will expect it to cover certain areas of your business—such as the product, market, and financial highlights, at the very least.

While you need to include what's necessary, you should also highlight areas that you believe will spark the reader's interest. Remember, you're telling the brief but convincing story of your business with this summary. Just be sure that you're able to back it up with the right details with the rest of your business plan."

(Tim Berry, "How to Write an Executive Summary", Bplans, https://www.bplans.com/business-planning/how-to-write/executive-summary/, 3/5/23)

>>> **fact or fiction**

Because the executive summary comes first in your plan, you may think you should write it first as well. Actually, you should write it last, after you've spent considerable time mulling over every other part of your plan. Only then will you truly be able to produce a summary of all that is there. Returning to the CliffsNotes analogy, it's impossible to summarize a book until the book is written.

A good rule of thumb for writing an effective and efficient business plan is to avoid repeating information. Brief is better and clearer, and needless repetition may annoy some readers and confuse others. Take extra care when writing your summary. You'll be glad you did.

Ultimately, you want the executive summary to be as strong as possible because it is also the first thing people read in your plan, and we all know the power of a strong first impression. This is where you want to wow people and make them think. This is like the coming attractions, or trailers, at the movie theater. You want that trailer to be enticing and bring the audience members back to see the film. Likewise, you want your readers to want to read your plan.

## Purposes of the Executive Summary

The executive summary has to perform a host of jobs. First and foremost, it should grab the reader's attention. It has to briefly hit the high points of your plan. It should point readers with questions requiring detailed responses to the full-length sections of your plan where they can get answers. It should ease the task of anybody whose job it is to read it, and it should make that task enjoyable by presenting an interesting and compelling account of your company.

The first question any investor has is, "How much?" followed closely by, "When will I recoup my investment?" Perceived risk and exit strategies are supportive information, and these in turn are supported by the quality of the management team and the proposed strategies.

It doesn't much matter whether you are presenting the plan to a family member, friend, banker, or sophisticated investors such as investment bankers or venture capitalists. They all need the same information. Concealing the amount and terms will only lessen your chances of a successful financing.

"The executive summary provides quick access to critical information from your more detailed business plan.

It is essential for informing anyone outside of your business. Many people—including investors and bankers—will only read your summary. Others will use it to decide if they should read the rest. For you, it is a snapshot of your business to reference when planning or revising your strategy.

Now if you're writing a business plan solely for internal use you may not need an executive summary. However, some internal plans—such as an annual operations plan or a strategic plan—benefit from having a summary.

It takes some effort to do a good summary, so if you don't have a business use in mind, don't do it."

(Tim Berry, "How to Write an Executive Summary", Bplans, https://www.bplans.com/business-planning/how-to-write/ executive-summary/, 3/5/23)

>>> **plan pointer**

Five minutes. This is how long an average reader will spend with your plan. If you can't convey the basics of your business in that time, your plan is in trouble. So make sure your summary, at least, can be read in that time and that it's as comprehensive as possible within that constraint. If you are using a deck, limit yourself to one slide and one minute of comments.

**Points to Include in an Executive Summary**

A suggested format for an executive summary:

1. The business idea and why it is necessary. (What problem does it solve?)
2. How much will it cost, and how much financing are you seeking?
3. What will the return be to the investor? Over what length of time?
4. What is the perceived risk level?
5. Where does your idea fit into the marketplace?
6. What is the management team?
7. What are the product and competitive strategies?
8. What is your marketing plan?
9. What is your exit strategy?

If you can address each of these in two or three sentences, you will have a twenty to twenty-seven sentence executive summary.

## What's the Big Idea?

Let's face it, every new and successful enterprise is the result of someone with an idea. People aren't going to finance you without knowing your idea. Sometimes the idea is so powerful that it generates a tremendous response right off the bat. This is unusual, but it does happen—it's when the reader stops you and says, "You don't have to tell me any more; I'm sold." More often, you'll need to explain why your idea has merit and how it can solve a common problem by making things easier, faster, or cheaper for the prospective customer(s).

Business ideas that no one has ever thought of are rare. So are new inventions. But new spins on old ideas are plentiful. Some of these are game changers, while others simply give consumers something new that solves a problem or makes some aspect of life easier. Then there are ideas that fall into the "same old, same old" category. No matter how brilliantly crafted, written, and presented your business plan is, it will be difficult to win your investors, and later customers, with an old idea that does NOT have a new twist. Therefore, you want to wow them first with your idea! If they're not interested, no matter what your financials are, they won't help.

## How Much Cash?

If you are using your plan as a financing proposal, and you probably are, put this information right up front. Are you seeking a loan, convertible debt, or equity investment? What terms, both in interest and length of loan, are you requesting? If equity, what is the probable exit strategy—and when will the exit strategy be executed?

Some readers will stop right here. That's fine. Other readers will appreciate your frankness. Being coy about amounts and terms will only harm your venture.

### Using the Cash

Provide a short explanation of how you'll use any financing you seek. Tell the investor why you need the money. Nobody wants to lend you money if they don't know exactly why you need it. It's not necessary to get into much detail here—just make it clear that you need it for x, y, and z. You don't have to justify every penny and wind up feeling obligated to ask for a loan of $23,558.36 because that's the exact price of everything you need. You should also let the reader know how the investment will help the company grow and/or increase its profits. Why else would you be seeking funding? The best use of somebody else's money is to buy or build something that will make more money, both for you and for that person.

## The Goals of Financiers

In your executive summary, consider the following:

> ▷ Friends and family want to get their money back someday but are not very interested in timing and returns.

❯ Bankers look for free cash flow to pay back the principal and interest of their loan. They also look closely at management experience and marketing. They may ask for collateral. By law they have to be conservative, that is, risk averse, so they are not great candidates for risky financing.

❯ Angel investors look for moderate rates of return, usually above the prime rate, plus some capital appreciation. They sometimes want to be involved at a hands-on level.

❯ Venture capitalists seek annual compound rates of return in the area of 35 to 50 percent per annum. They seldom want to go longer than three to five years to cash out. They always want to know what the exit strategy is.

You may have special considerations to address in any given plan, depending on its target. For instance, you may know or suspect that one of the conditions of getting a loan from your parents is that you employ your black-sheep cousin. Be sure your summary of management has a slot—Director of Ephemera might work—for that unworthy individual.

Don't forget yourself: It's a rare company that doesn't have any investment from the entrepreneur or entrepreneurs who started it.

---

### ❯❯❯ plan pointer

Assessing your own strengths and weaknesses is a lot harder than assessing others' good and bad points, right? So when it comes time to select your best features, it's also time to solicit feedback from others. Ask people whose opinions you trust, such as colleagues, associates, and peers, whether your assessment of your idea is off base or on target.

---

## Who Will Own What?

When a business starts generating profits and plowing them back into the firm, value can build rapidly. Even if you aren't in an industry likely to purchase buildings or patent valuable technology, the business derives value from the fact that it can generate profits into the future.

Because your business is valuable, spell out who owns what. If you have many equity investors coupled with a pile of creditors, this can get pretty complicated.

For the summary section of your plan, a basic description such as "Ownership of the company will be divided so that each of the four original partners owns 25 percent" will suffice. If you have to negotiate details of exactly what any equity investors will get, there's time to do that later. For now, you just want to give people an idea of how the ownership will be divided.

## Give It a Happy Ending

If you tell a story in the summary, give it a happy ending. Although it's your duty to fully disclose to investors any significant risk factors, you can save that for later. The summary is the place to put your best foot forward, to talk up the upside and downplay the downside.

As always, accentuating the positive doesn't mean exaggeration or lying. If there is a really important, unusual risk factor in your plan—such as that one certain big customer has to make a huge order for the whole plan to work—then you will want to mention that in your summary. But run-of-the-mill risks like unexpected competition or customer reluctance can be ignored here.

Paint a convincing portrait of an opportunity so compelling that only a dullard would not recognize it and desire to take part in it.

### Show Why You Care

No matter if you're sharing your plan with an investor, customer, or team member, your plan needs to show that you're passionate, dedicated, and that you actually care about your business and the plan. You can also discuss the mistakes that you've learned from, list the problems that you're hoping to solve, describe your values, and establish what makes you stand out from the competition.

By explaining why you care about your business, you create an emotional connection with your readers so that they'll support you, your team, and your organization.

## Company Description

If your company is complex, you'll need a separate section inside the plan with a heading like "Company Description" to describe its many product lines, locations, services, or whatever else it is that makes it a little too complicated to deal with quickly. In any event, you provide a brief description, no longer than a few sentences, of your company in the executive summary. And for many firms, this is an adequate basic description of their company. Here are some one- or two-sentence (mock) company descriptions:

- John's Handball Hut is the Hamish Valley's leading purveyor of handball equipment and clothing.
- Boxes Boxes Boxes Inc. will provide the people of the metropolitan area with a comprehensive source for packing materials, containers, and other supplies for the do-it-yourself move.
- Salem Segway Witch Tours offers tourists the only Segway tours of the infamous home of the seventeenth century witch trials.

## Optional Information

The following items are not a necessity in your business plan: mission statement and corporate vision. If you have honed either down to a clear and concise sentence, by all means, use it in your plan.

## Mission Statement

A mission statement is a sentence or two describing the company's function, market, competitive advantages, and the business goals and philosophies.

Many mission statements communicate what your business is about and should include a description of what makes you different from everybody else in your field. Mission statements have a place in a plan: They help investors and other interested parties get a grip on what makes your company special. A mission statement should be clearly written. Here are some (again, mock) examples:

- ⟫ River City Roadsters buys, restores, and resells classic American cars from the 1950s and 1960s to antique-auto buffs throughout central Missouri.
- ⟫ Captain Curio is the Jersey Shore's leading antique store, catering to high-quality interior decorators and collectors across the tristate area.
- ⟫ August Appleton, Esq., provides low-cost legal services to personal-injury, workers' compensation, and age-discrimination plaintiffs in Houston's Fifth Ward.

## Corporate Vision

A mission statement describes the goals and objectives you could "reasonably" expect to accomplish. A small software company whose mission statement included the goal of "putting Microsoft out of business" would be looked upon as foolishly naive.

In a vision statement, however, just those sorts of grandiose, galactic-scale images are perfectly appropriate. When you "vision"—to borrow the management consultant's trick of turning nouns into verbs—you imagine the loftiest heights you could scale, not the next step or several steps on the ladder.

Does a vision statement even have a place in a business plan? You could argue that it doesn't, especially because many include personal components such as "to love every minute of my work and always feel I'm doing my best." But many investors deeply respect visionary entrepreneurs. So, if you feel you have a compelling vision, there's no reason not to share it in your plan.

## Extract the Essence

The key to the executive summary is to pick out the best aspects of every part of your plan. In other words, you want to extract the essence. Instead of describing everyone in your company, talk only about your key managers. Instead of talking about all your products, mention only the major ones or discuss only product lines instead of individual products. It's a highlight reel, so to speak.

### Article Tools and Summarizing the Summary

Within the overall outline of the business plan, the executive summary will follow the title page. The summary should tell the reader what you are planning to do. All too often, the business owner's desires are buried and lost when the reader scrolls through. Clearly state what you are planning to do (your ideas) and what you are seeking in the summary.

The statement should be kept short and businesslike, ideally no more than half a page. It could be longer, depending on how complicated the use of funds may be, but the summary of a business plan, like the summary of a loan application, is generally no more than one page. Within that space you'll need to provide a synopsis of the entire business plan. Key elements that should be included are:

▷ *Financial requirements.* Clearly states the capital needed to start or expand the business. Detail how the capital will be used and the equity, if any, that will be provided for funding. If the loan for initial capital will be based on security instead of equity within the company, you should also specify the source of collateral.

▷ *Business concept.* Describes the business, its product(s), and the market it will serve. It should point out just exactly what will be sold, to whom, and why the business will hold a competitive advantage.

⟩ *Financial features.* Highlights the important financial points of the business including sales, profits, cash flows, and return on investment.

⟩ *Current business position.* Furnishes relevant information about the company, its legal form of operation, when it was formed, the principal owners, and key personnel.

⟩ *Major achievements.* Details any developments within the company that are essential to the success of the business. Major achievements include items like patents, prototypes, location of a facility, any crucial contracts that need to be in place for product development, or results from any test marketing that has been conducted.

When writing your statement of purpose, don't waste words. If the executive summary is eight pages, nobody's going to read it because it will be very clear that the business, no matter what its merits, won't be a good investment because the principals are indecisive and don't really know what they want. Make it easy for the reader to realize at first glance both your needs and capabilities.

## Chapter 7 Summary

In the management section of your plan, you describe who will run the company. This may be no more than a simple paragraph noting that you'll be the only executive and describing your background. Or it may be a major section in the plan, consisting of an organizational chart describing interrelationships among every department and manager in the company, plus bios of all key executives.

Time and again, financiers utter some variation of the following statement: "I don't invest in ideas; I invest in people." Although there's some question as to whether this is the whole story—investors certainly prefer capable people with good ideas to inept people with good ideas—there's no doubt that you, and the people who run your company, will receive considerable scrutiny from financiers as well as from customers, suppliers, and anyone else with an interest in your plan. People are, after all, a company's most important asset. Not adequately addressing this issue in a business plan is a serious failing. Luckily, it's one of the easiest parts.

What you'll learn from this chapter:

- Why you should talk about yourself and your management team
- How to explain your hiring projections
- How to add and retain key employees
- If and when you should get a board of directors or advisors
- How to find outside professionals to help you
- Ways to discuss licenses and certifications you need

# Management Makes Money

## All about You

They say "pay yourself first" when you run a business. It's important when doing a business plan to feature yourself first. After all, you are the person, the entrepreneur, behind the business venture, and it is you who will have to put your neck on the line, answer the hard questions, and take the criticism—as well as the praise and acclaim, should there be some.

Before you can impress people with your management team, it's important to let your readers know who is at the helm and who is selecting the management team. You, therefore, have to let them know your background, including your vision, your credentials, and why you chose the management team you did.

A business follows the lead of the founder, and as such, you need to briefly explain what is expected of this management team and the role you see it, as a group, playing in the future of this business.

## Your Managers

Identifying your managers is about presenting what they bring to the table. You can provide this by describing them in terms of the following characteristics:

> *Education.* Impressive educational credentials among company managers provide strong reasons for an investor or other plan reader to feel good about your company. Use your judgment in deciding what educational background to include and how to emphasize it. If you're starting a fine restaurant, for example, and your chef graduated at the top of her class from the Culinary Institute of America, play that front and center. If you're starting a courier service and your partner has an anthropology degree from a little-known school, mention it but don't make a big deal out of it.

> *Employment.* Prior work experience in a related field is something many investors look for. If you've spent ten years in management in the retail men's apparel business before opening a tuxedo outlet, an investor can feel confident that you know what you're doing. Likewise, you'll want to explain the key, appropriate positions of your team members. Describe any relevant jobs in terms of job title, years of experience, names of employers, and so on. But remember, this isn't a resume. You can feel free to skim over or omit any irrelevant experience. You do not have to provide exact dates of employment.

> *Skills.* A title is one thing; what you learn while holding it is another. In addition to pointing out that you were a district sales manager for a stereo equipment wholesaler, you should describe your responsibilities and the skills you honed while fulfilling them. Again, list the skills that your management team has that pertain to

this business. A great cook may have incredible accounting skills, but that doesn't matter in the kitchen of the new restaurant.

Each time you mention skills that you or a member of your management team has spent years acquiring at another company, it will be another reason for an investor to believe you can do it at your own company.

》》 **buzzword**

Functional organization is a term describing a company or other entity with a structure that divides authority and reporting along functions such as marketing or finance. These functions cross product lines and other boundaries.

》 *Accomplishments.* Dust off your plaques and trot out your calculator for this one. If you or one of your team members has been awarded patents, achieved record sales gains, or once opened an unbelievable number of new stores in the space of a year, now's the time to talk about it.

Don't brag. Just be factual and remember to quantify. If, for example, you have twelve patents, your sales manager had five years of thirty percent annual sales gains, and you personally oversaw the grand openings of forty-two stores in eleven months, this is the stuff investors and others reading your business plan will want to see. Investors are looking to back impressive winners, and quantifiable results speak strongly to businesspeople of all stripes.

》》 **buzzword**

Line organization describes an organization divided by product lines, means of production, industries served, and so on. Each line may have its own support staff for the various functions.

》 *Personal.* Who cares about personal stuff? Isn't this business? Sure, but investors want to know with whom they're dealing in terms of the personal side, too. Personal information on each member of your management team may include age, city of residence, notable charitable or community activities, and, last but far from least, personal motivation for joining the company. Investors like to see vigorous, committed, involved people in the companies they back. Mentioning one or two of the relevant personal details of your key managers may help investors feel they know what they're getting into, especially in today's increasingly transparent business climate.

Many businesses contain unique functions. For example, only product companies such as software publishers have product testing departments. List functions that are unique to your company under the "Other" category.

**Whom Else Do You Include in Your Plan?**

If you're the only manager, this question is an easy one. But what if you have a pretty well-established organization already? Should you mention everyone down to shop foremen or stop with the people who are on your executive committee? The answer is, probably neither. Instead think about your managers in terms of the important functions of your business.

In deciding the scope of the management section of your plan, consider the following business functions, and make sure you've explained who will handle those that are important to your enterprise:

- Accounting
- Advertising
- Distribution
- Finance
- Human Resources
- Legal
- Training

- Marketing
- Operations
- Production
- Purchasing
- Sales
- Technical Operations

## What Does Each Person Do?

There's more to a job than a title. A director in one organization is a high and mighty individual, whereas in another company a person bearing the same title is practically nobody. And many industries have unique job titles, such as managing editor, creative director, and junior accountant level II, that have no counterparts in other industries.

In a longer plan, when you give your management team's background and describe their titles, don't stop there. Go on and tell the reader exactly what each member of the management team will be expected to do in the company. This may be especially important in a startup, in which not every position is filled from the start. If your marketing work is going to be handled by the CFO until you get a little further down the road, let readers know this up front. You certainly can't expect them to figure that out on their own.

In a shorter business plan, or miniplan, choose those people most vital to your business. If you are opening a martial arts studio, the instructors, or lead instructor, are significant, as is the software developer in a new software company. While you have room to describe these people in more detail in a longer plan, in the shorter miniplans, just use one defining sentence for your top five people.

## Expanding Your Team

If you do have significant holes in your management team, you'll want to describe your plans for filling them. You may say, for example, "Marketing duties are being handled on a temporary basis by the vice president for finance. Once sales have reached the $500,000 per month level, approximately six months after startup, a dedicated vice president of marketing will be retained to fulfill that function."

In some cases, particularly if you're in a really shaky startup and you need solid talent, you may have to describe in some detail your plans for luring a hotshot industry expert to your fledgling enterprise. Then, briefly describe your ideal candidate. For a miniplan you may write "We plan to hire a marketing VP who excels in reaching our 20–29 target market."

## Hiring and Projections

One of the beauties of being an entrepreneur, as opposed to a solo practitioner or freelancer, is that you can leverage the activities and skills of all the people whom you employ. This is one of the secrets to building a personal fortune. And it's one you can use even if you didn't happen to be born with a silver spoon in your mouth or an oil well in your backyard.

To use a simple example of the profit power of people, say you start a public relations firm. You bill clients $120 an hour, plus other office expenses, for services provided by your account executives (AEs). You pay your staff $60 an hour, including benefits. Before expenses for rent and other overhead items, then, you clear $30 for every hour one of your AEs bills. If you can grow your AE staff very large (and generate enough business to keep them busy), it can leverage your earnings very rapidly indeed. Of course, you have to train people to work autonomously and take control of their tasks so that you do not have to spend time managing their every move—otherwise, you're losing money by using your time in an unproductive manner.

The decision of how many people you want to manage is entirely up to you. It depends on the time commitment that you cannot make for doing other tasks or the need to perform skills that aren't your strengths. Part of hiring other people is to have them handle aspects of the business that you cannot or should not be doing. After all, we have different personalities, interests, and passions. There are very few one-person businesses unless you are including independent contractors. Businesses are run by teams of people, from two or three to thousands, and team members excel in a wide range of areas. You also need to factor in how much you expect to grow. Some entrepreneurs want to retain a small, easy-to-manage business, while others want to build an empire.

Let's say, for example, you wish to add a second shift at your small factory manufacturing smartphone cases. Your day shift employs ten factory floor workers plus a supervisor. Can you just hire eleven people and start running the swing shift? Not necessarily. It may be that two of those workers only work part-time on the production line, spending much of their day helping the shipping department process incoming materials and outgoing orders. Two more may devote several hours to routine maintenance procedures that won't have to be done twice a day even when a second shift is added. So your real needs may be for seven production workers and a supervisor—a savings of 20 percent in your projected staffing increase. It's decisions like this that easily can make the difference between a highly profitable operation and one barely scraping by. Figure 7.1 can help here.

"For many businesses, personnel is the largest expense, so it's important to think through the forecast and make adjustments to the timing of planned hiring based on your revenue projections, profitability, and the cash you have available to meet payroll obligations.

Of course, you'll also want to think about how your business is organized and what the management structure will look like. You can use tools such as an organizational chart to help figure out your personnel plan and then add that to your business plan."

(Noah Parsons, "How to Forecast Personnel Costs in 3 Steps", Bplans, https://www.bplans.com/business-planning/how-to-write/financial-plan/personnel-forecast/, 3/8/23)

## Strategic Hiring Questions

To help you in your strategic staffing projections, consider these factors:

1.  What are your key business objectives?

    (*Hint*: These may be things such as increasing sales or reducing costs. The idea is to make sure that your hiring decisions fit your strategy. If, for example, geographically expanding your retail store chain is a primary objective, a staffing plan will have to include managers for each new location.)

2.  What skills will your employees need?

3.  What new skills will current employees need to possess? (*Hint*: You may find you are better off with fewer workers who are more highly trained or have different skill sets.)

4.  Which of these skills are central to your business—your core competencies?

    (*Hint*: You may want to outsource peripheral functions. Accounting, legal matters, and human resources are frequently outsourced by companies whose main business is elsewhere and who find it doesn't make sense to spend the effort to attract and retain skilled employees in these areas.)

5.  List the jobs and job descriptions of the people it will take to provide these skills.

    (*Hint*: The idea here is to identify the employees whose job titles may mask their actual function in the organization so you can figure out how many people, and what type of people, you really need to include.)

6.  Determine how many people you will be hiring and what your budget will be for these positions. Will there be any job sharing?

    (*Hint*: Make sure your salaries are commensurate with the going rates in your region. If you can pay more, you can attract a higher level of employees. If you pay less, then try to find nonmonetary benefits that you can also offer, such as telecommuting, which saves employees time and money on getting to and from work each day.)

Now you should be able to make an accurate projection of not only how many but what kind of people you need to achieve your long-term objectives.

**Figure 7.1.** Strategic Hiring Worksheet

---

## Adding and Retaining Key Employees

If you want your business to grow, you'll want to have key employees that share your vision and goals. Sometimes you will find an established individual, like a highly acclimated chef for your restaurant or an art director with years of experience for your company. In other cases, you may not know when you bring someone on board what the future holds, but you believe she has what it takes to become a key employee. These are individuals that you can envision moving up the path of ascension. Either way, you should make it clear in your business plan which key positions you want to fill and how you plan to go about finding the people to fill those roles.

Of course, the economy will factor into your decision on whom to hire and how much you can afford to pay them. In a struggling economy, more highly skilled employees will be seeking work, but you may not be in a position to risk high salaries. In such instances you may opt for trial periods before committing to full-time salaries. You may also look for independent contractors for key positions. Remember, it is much easier to find skilled people in various aspects of business than it is to learn everything yourself. When the economy is going well, however, you will have to up the ante to bring on key employees because there is more competition. Then there is your plan to hold onto key employees, which is important to include in your business plan.

>>> **plan pointer**

An organizational chart graphically sorts your company into its major functional departments—finance, administration, marketing, production, and so on. It's the quickest, clearest way to say who is in charge of what and who reports to whom.

The things that make employees want to come to work for you and stay vary. For employees, choosing whom to work for is a highly personal decision. That's why it's crucial to understand the individual needs of your key employees so that you can give them exactly what they want. If you offer only a higher salary to an employee whose most important concern is that she works at a job offering flexible hours so she can care for an elderly parent, then you probably won't retain that employee.

Here are some common concerns that drive employment decisions:

▷ *Benefits.* Paid holidays and sick leave, health insurance, and retirement plans such as 401(k)s are among the benefits listed as most desirable by employees.

▷ *Compensation.* Salary, bonuses, stock options, profit sharing, and auto mileage allowances are among the most important compensation issues to employees.

▷ *Miscellaneous.* On-site childcare, flexible schedules, telecommuting, paid memberships to business groups, and health perks such as yoga classes or free medical screenings are also important to employees.

---

### ⧽⧽ buzzword

Outsourcing is a key strategy for startups. If you've ever fired your bookkeeper and started sending payroll to a service, you've outsourced. Basically, you are using a service instead of your own employee(s) to do a specific task. Outsourcing can save time and money for support staff jobs and add flexibility in production staffing. Again, it shows that you are watching the bottom line closely and not hiring people full-time for part-time duties.

---

Your business plan should consider the above issues and describe the inducements you will offer key employees to encourage them to stay. Especially in a small company, an investor is likely to be very leery of a plan that appears to be based on the capabilities of a handful of employees unless the business owner has clearly given a lot of thought to keeping these important people on board.

**plan of action**

*The Perfect Hire* (Entrepreneur Press), by Katherine Graham-Leviss, quickly, economically, and precisely advises you on finding, hiring, and keeping the best employees.

The above list is by no means comprehensive, however. Employee needs are as complex as humanity. One person may stay because she likes the view out her window on a high floor; somebody in an identical office may leave because heights make him nervous. One of the most important needs, especially for highly motivated employees, is maintaining a constant atmosphere of learning, challenge, and advancement. If you can find a way to let your employees grow as your company does, and feel a sense of ownership and inclusion, they're likely to be more conscientious and motivated.

## Board of Directors or Advisors

A board of directors gives you access to expertise, provided you choose them wisely, but at the cost of giving up control of the business to them. Technically, the officers of a corporation report to the board of directors, who bear the ultimate responsibility for the proper management of the company. Most boards will have financial, marketing, and organizational experts. Such a board lends great credibility to a company. Board members can provide more than oversight and sounding board skills; they provide a wealth of contacts and referrals.

A board of advisors is a less formal entity. You can have the same kind of people on an advisory board, but you don't report to them and they don't have the same power as a board of directors. Beware of creating a rubber-stamp board. You need the variety and breadth of experience and skills a board (of directors or advisors) brings to the table. Running a business is hard enough without adding an echo chamber. Your board should be able to challenge your thinking, help you solve knotty problems, and even change management if necessary.

Your board members, and their reasons for being included, should be a brief part of your longer business plan, not the miniplan.

---

>>> **plan pointer**

Keep in mind that there are many consultants out there, some of whom are invaluable and others who take in information and regurgitate it back to you in some other form. Choose wisely.

---

## Outside Professionals

Some of the most important people who'll do work for you won't work for you. Your attorney, your accountant, and your insurance broker are all crucial members of your team. A good professional in one of these slots can go a long way toward helping you succeed. The same may be true, to a lesser extent, for real estate brokers, management consultants, benefits consultants, computer consultants, trainers, and both creative and IT help.

Your business plan should reassure readers that you have your bases covered in these important professional positions. Readers don't necessarily want to see an attorney on staff. It's fine that you merely state that you retain the services of an attorney in private practice on an as-needed basis. In fact, often it's more prudent to show that you are not spending money on full-timers that you don't need.

You don't even need to name the firm you're retaining, although a prestigious name here may generate some reflected respect for you. For instance, if your firm is audited by a prominent firm instead of a local one-man accounting shop, then by all means play it up. Few things are more comforting to an investor than the knowledge that this investment's disbursement will be monitored regularly and carefully by an expert.

Investors want profit. They don't just give money to people they like or admire. But it's also true that if they don't like, admire, or at least respect the people running your company, they're likely to look elsewhere. The management section of your plan is where you tell them about the human side of the equation. You can't control your readers' responses to that, but you owe it to them and to yourself to provide the information.

**Checking It Twice**

Here are some common licenses and certifications you may need. Check this list to see if there's anything you may have forgotten:

- Business license
- DBA (doing business as) or fictitious name statement
- Federal Employer ID Number
- Local tax forms
- Sales tax permit or seller's permit
- Health inspection certificate
- Fire inspection certificate
- Patent filings
- Trademark registration
- Zoning variance

Many of these forms and certificates will take days, weeks, months, or longer to arrive after you request them from the appropriate parties. So don't wait until the last minute to do so. Nothing is more frustrating than sitting in a ready-to-open store, with employees on the clock and interest charges on inventory and fixtures ticking away as well, but unable to serve customers because you don't have your sales tax permit.

## Licenses and Certifications

Some paperwork is just paperwork, and some paperwork is essential. Every business must file tax returns, and most businesses need certain licenses and certifications to do business. Your plan should take notice, however briefly, of the fact that you have received or applied for any necessary licenses and certificates. If you don't mention the subject, some plan readers will assume all is hunky-dory. Others, however, may suspect the omission means you haven't thought about it or are having trouble getting the paperwork in order. Addressing those concerns now is a worthwhile idea.

Aside from the usual business licenses and tax forms, there are any number of certificates and notices you may require, depending on circumstances. Owners of buildings must have their elevators inspected regularly and, in some cities, post the safety inspection record in public. Plumbers must be licensed in many states. Even New York City hot dog vendors must be licensed by the city before they can unfurl their carts' colorful umbrellas.

For some businesses, their certification or occupational license is essentially what they sell. Think of a CPA. A lot of people sell accounting services. When you go to a CPA, you're paying for the probity and skill represented by the CPA designation, not just another accountant. You're basically buying those initials. FYI: Patents, trademarks, and other signs of creativity and resourcefulness that are registered or licensed can be impressive.

## Consult an Attorney

As you begin to create a business plan for your company, sound legal advice is important. Attorneys are an integral part of strategic business planning because they offer the guidance necessary to ensure short- and long-term stability. Proper planning and organization in the beginning will lessen the likelihood of problems arising as your business develops.

Prior to creating a business plan, five issues should be reviewed with your attorney:

1. What type of entity will the business use?
2. How will you raise money to fund the business endeavors?
3. How will you staff the business, and what compensation and benefits will you provide to your employees?
4. Does the business have important intellectual property or proprietary information, and if so, how will it be protected?
5. How will doing business abroad be handled?

Attention to detail in each of these areas is imperative in creating a successful strategic business plan.

In establishing your company's legal entity, consider the advantages and disadvantages of each type—sole proprietorship, partnership, C corporation, S corporation, and limited liability company (LLC). Choosing the right business entity is imperative in a successful business venture because there are many tax and nontax implications. A good lawyer can help you determine which entity would be best for your particular company and situation.

Financing a business requires knowledge of the laws governing the ways in which companies may raise money. For instance, when taking on investors, whether they are family and friends, angel investors, or venture capital investors, there are securities law issues that may inhibit the way in which money may be accepted.

An important question to ask is, "How do I raise money and not violate the law?" Legal professionals can guide you in your planning process to ensure that your company will not violate the laws regarding financing.

Determining staffing needs is yet another necessary component of a strong business plan. A lawyer can develop contracts and other detailed documents important in the hiring process. Salary issues need to be determined, too—for example, will your employees be paid hourly, or will they be salaried? Other considerations include incentive plans and employee benefits, such as health insurance, retirement plans, and stock options. An employee handbook can also be a useful tool to set up a foundation for employee policies and procedures. All issues regarding employees typically require a lawyer's involvement to avoid the specific liabilities that your company may face. In fact, your corporate attorney may not be the right person for labor law, so you may need to discuss hiring issues, including handbooks and even employee forms, with a labor lawyer.

Intellectual property and proprietary information can provide a company with a needed competitive advantage. Therefore, because of the potential importance of intellectual property and proprietary information, an attorney should be consulted to ensure that it is properly protected. Ensuring all employees sign proprietary information and invention agreements is one step in protecting your company's intellectual property and proprietary information. Obtaining patents or federal registration of the company's trademarks is also critical to proper protection.

Another aspect of the business plan should include how relationships with customers and suppliers will be established and what the terms of the legal relationship will be with them. The necessary question to ask and answer is whether standard terms and conditions will apply or whether each relationship will be contracted individually. In addition is the need to decide whether any of the Uniform Commercial Code (UCC) provisions will be overridden. Certain UCC provisions, such as implied warranties, will govern unless specifically disclaimed.

To find a competent attorney for your company, seek referrals from other business managers. It's important to meet with more than one firm to determine which one is best for your particular company. Look for experience in your industry, as well as chemistry between you and the firm. Keep in mind that you may need more than one attorney to cover all the different bases. A good law firm, housing lawyers with different specialties, such as contracts, labor, taxes, and so on, may be beneficial to your needs.

Don't be afraid to talk about fees. It is important to know what you're paying for to determine if you're getting your money's worth.

Successful businesses deal with a variety of laws and regulations on a daily basis, so it is important to hire an attorney who specializes in your business and can help facilitate the growth of your company. Consulting an attorney before drafting your business plan will result in a more well-thought-out and better drafted business plan. This will lessen the likelihood of problems as the company grows, saving both time and money. Through knowledge and experience, a good lawyer can efficiently aid in the creation of a successful business plan.

## Chapter 8 Summary

Every business has something to sell, and the product section is where you tell readers what it is you're selling. (For simplicity's sake, the term "product" is used to refer to both products and services unless otherwise indicated.) This is clearly a very important section of your plan. Even if you have assembled a brilliant managerial team, or have strong financial underpinnings, unless you have something to sell or at least plans to develop something new, you don't really have a business at all. Business is about providing people with something they need. Your business should solve a problem, make life easier, expedite a process, or even simply entertain, but you need to be selling something to have a business.

Although many businesses are founded to develop new, never-before-seen products, they're still built around a product, even though it may not exist at the moment. And even for these development-stage enterprises, it's just as important to describe the planned-for product and make a presentation that illustrates what people can expect.

What you'll learn from this chapter:

- » How to explain what your product and/or service is
- » How to communicate what makes what you offer worthwhile
- » Ways to ensure that you don't expose yourself to risk
- » How to understand what you need to know about products

# What Do You Sell?

## What Is Your Product or Service?

It's easy to talk eloquently about a product you believe in. Some highly marketing-oriented businesses, in fact, are built as much on the ability to wax rhapsodic about a product as they are on the ability to buy or source compelling products to begin with. Think of J. Peterman, the catalog operation that became famous—and highly successful—by selling prosaic products with the help of romantic, overblown advertising copy, prior to going bankrupt in 1999.

It's important in your plan to be able to build a convincing case for the product or service upon which your business will be built. The product description section is where you do that.

In this section, describe your product in terms of several characteristics, including cost, features, distribution, target market, competition, and production concerns. Figure 8.1 can help you define your product.

> "Many experts recommend introducing your business plan with definitions of the problem that your business solves and the solution your business offers.
>
> That's called "problem and solution," and it's quite common and quite useful—but it's also too often an opportunity wasted.
>
> Don't just describe the problem and solution. Make people care."
>
> (Tim Berry,"How to Create a Convincing Problem and Solution Statement", Bplans, https://www.bplans.com/business-planning/how-to-write/products-services/define-problem/, 3/8/23)

## Product Description Worksheet

Features describe the make, shape, form, or appearance of a product, the characteristics that you use to describe products. These features convey benefits to the customer. Benefits (perceived benefits) are the emotional or other end results that your product or service provides that customer, the satisfaction or fulfillment of needs that a customer receives from your products or services. In the famous phrase "My factories make cosmetics, we sell hope," cosmetics are the products, hope is the benefit.

| Product Description | Features | Benefit Conveyed | Importance for My Product |
|---|---|---|---|
| Physical characteristics: | Shape | | |
| | Color | | |
| | Size | | |
| | Weight | | |
| | Fresh | | |
| Specified characteristics: | Made by . . . | | |
| | Imported from . . . | | |
| | Price | | |
| | New! Improved! | | |
| | Location | | |
| | Delivery | | |
| Follow-up service | Availability | | |
| | Durability | | |
| | Reliability | | |
| | Service | | |
| | Ease of use | | |
| | Tech support | | |
| | Used by | | |

**Figure 8.1.** Product Description Worksheet

Here are a few sample product descriptions:

> *Street Beat* is a new type of portable electronic rhythm machine used to create musical backgrounds for street dances, fairs, concerts, picnics, sporting events, and other outdoor productions. The product is less costly than a live rhythm section and offers better sound quality than competing systems. Its combination of features will appeal to sports promoters, fair organizers, and charitable and youth organizations.

> *Troubleshooting Times* is the only monthly magazine for the nation's 6,000 owners of electronics repair shops. It provides timely news of industry trends, service product reviews, and consumer product service tips written in a language service shop owners can understand.

> *HOBO, the Home Business Organization,* provides business consulting services to entrepreneurs who work out of their homes. The group connects home business owners with experts who have extensive experience counseling home business owners in management, finance, marketing, and lifestyle issues. Unlike entrepreneurial peer groups, which charge members for attending sessions whether or not they receive useful advice, HOBO will guarantee its services, asking home business owners to pay only if they derive solid benefit from the service.

A business plan product description has to be less image conscious than an advertising brochure but more appealing than a simple spec sheet. You don't want to give the appearance of trying to dazzle readers with a glitzy product sales pitch filled with a lot of hype. On the other hand, you want to give them a sampling of how you are going to position and promote the product.

### ⟫ plan pointer

No ideas to differentiate your product? Steal someone else's. That is, combine your product with another to create something new. Dry cleaners do this when they offer coupons for the neighborhood pizza parlor—which gives out cleaning coupons with each pie. It's called cooperative marketing.

A business plan product description is not only concerned with consumer appeal. Issues of manufacturability are of paramount concern to plan readers, who may have seen any number of plans describing exciting products that, in the end, proved impossible to design and build economically.

If your product or service has special features that will make it easy to build and distribute, say so. For instance, the portable rhythm machine maker should point out in the business plan that the devices will be constructed using new special-purpose integrated circuits derived from military applications, which will vastly increase durability and quality while reducing costs. Figure 8.2 on page 139 shows potential unique selling propositions that any product or service may be able to provide. Look at the list and ask yourself what your product has to offer buyers in each category.

---

### ⟫ buzzword

Unique selling proposition is a term for whatever it is that makes you different from and better than the competition in the eyes of your customers. It's why they buy from you instead of from someone else.

---

## What Makes It Worthwhile?

A product description is more than a mere listing of product features. You have to highlight your product's most compelling characteristics, such as low cost or uniquely high quality, that will make it stand out in the marketplace and attract buyers willing to pay your price. Even the simplest product has a number of unique potential selling strengths.

Many of the common unique selling strengths are seemingly contradictory. How can both mass popularity and exclusive distribution be strengths? The explanation is that it depends on your market and what its buyers want.

- ⟫ *Features.* If your product is faster, bigger, or smaller, or comes in more colors, sizes, and configurations than others on the market, you have a powerful selling strength. In fact, if you can't offer some combination of features that sets you apart, you'll have difficulty writing a convincing plan.

▷ *Price.* Everybody wants to pay less for a product. If you can position yourself as the low-cost provider (and make money at these rock-bottom prices), you have a powerful selling advantage. Conversely, high-priced products may appeal to many markets for their better quality and high-end value. People with discerning tastes want quality and do not buy based solely on price points, so saving money is not always the issue. Price is also dependent on other issues such as service. People will pay more for good customer service.

▷ *Time Savings.* People buy products to help them expedite a process. If yours is faster and can help your customers get out of the office and on their way home more quickly, they want it. Today, everyone is looking to save time, so products and services that help people do that are valuable.

▷ *Ease of Transport.* The mobile world has taken over. People are using their mobile phones to go online as much if not more than their laptops. How mobile is your product? Today's consumers like to take things with them—they want apps and gadgets that are portable.

▷ *Availability.* Typically, the more easily accessible your products are the better it is for business. In most cases, you want to have products and services that people can get quickly. Today, thanks to the internet, you no longer need brick-and-mortar locations in many communities. Scarcity, however, can also generate a higher demand, so you may have a marketing plan to release products at intervals and let the demand—and the desire—build. Scarcity doesn't mean that you will be running out anytime soon. For service providers, availability means a good location or locations that are easy to get to.

## Unique Selling Proposition Worksheet

When you've explained the selling propositions associated with your product in each of these categories, give each one a score from one to ten based on your evaluation of how convincing a case you can make for that being a unique selling proposition. The one or two strengths with the highest scores will be your candidates for inclusion in business plan product description.

| Features | |
|---|---|
| For products: | |
| | Price |
| | Time savings |
| | Ease of transport (mobility) |
| | Availability |
| | Cutting edge / new |
| | Training and support |
| | Financing |
| | Other |
| | |
| For the service providers: | |
| | Customer service |
| | Reputation |
| | Knowledge |
| | Experience |
| | Fast delivery |
| | Endorsements |
| | Other |

Figure 8.2. Unique Selling Proposition Worksheet

>>> **plan pitfall**

Don't count on getting your product into a major retailer on its own merits. The glut of tens of thousands of new products introduced annually, combined with the existing plethora of more than 30,000 products stocked by a typical supermarket, puts retailers in the driver's seat. They demand—and get from almost all new product makers—slotting fees, which are simply payments for the right to be on store shelves. The same goes for big online retailers like Amazon.

> *Cutting Edge / New.* If you have something to offer that is not on the market, this is a major selling point or competitive edge. Get out there and patent it, market it, and sell it before someone comes along and steals your thunder. You can also utilize technology to build upon products or services you already provide, such as an app.

> *Training and Support.* These are components of service that have become increasingly important, particularly for high-technology products. For many sophisticated software products and electronic devices, a seller who can't provide tech support to buyers will have no chance of success.

> *Financing.* Whether you "tote the note" and guarantee credit to anyone, offer innovative leasing, do buybacks, or have other financing alternatives, you'll find that giving people different, more convenient ways to pay can lend your product a convincing strength.

> *Customer Service.* Excellent service is perhaps the most important thing you can add to any product or service today. In a world where word travels fast through social media, you want to provide top-notch customer service. The shoe giant Zappos has built its reputation by providing excellent customer service. Make this a top priority.

**▷▷▷ plan pointer**

Tell people about what you sell. Your website, your packaging, and your marketing campaign should let people know what to expect when they purchase your products. Social media and Facebook pages should also have a lot written about your company and your product. And in case you receive social media comments that are not always favorable, you can address such negative comments in a polite manner. Savvy shoppers are reading more and more about what they intend on buying—so give them something positive to talk about.

▷ *Reputation.* Why do people pay $10,000 for a Rolex? The Rolex reputation is the reason. At its most extreme, reputation can literally keep you in business, as is the case with many companies, such as IBM and Walmart, whose well-developed reputations have tided them over in hard times.

▷ *Knowledge.* Your knowledge and the means you have of imparting that to customers is an important part of your total offering. Retailers of auto parts, home improvement supplies, and all sorts of other goods have found that simply having knowledgeable salespeople who know how to replace the water pump in a '95 Chevy will lure customers in and encourage them to buy.

▷ *Experience.* "We've been there. We've done thousands of installations like yours, and there's no doubt we can make this one work as well." Nothing could be more soothing to a skeptical sales prospect than to learn that the seller has vast experience at what he's doing. If you have ample experience, make it part of your selling proposition.

▷ *Fast Delivery.* Nobody wants to wait for anything anymore. If you can offer overnight shipping, on-site service, or 24/7 availability, it can turn an otherwise unremarkable product or service into a very attractive one.

▷ *Endorsements.* There's a reason Peyton Manning makes millions of dollars a year from endorsements. People want to relate to Peyton and share his aura, if only obliquely.

---

 **fact or fiction**

Don't make assumptions when you're looking at a new product or service idea. For instance, you might think that horseshoers are an endangered breed in the automobile era. Actually, the leisure and sport horse industry is thriving, and there are more farriers active today than when horses were the main mode of transport. Just because something seems out of fashion doesn't mean you're out of luck.

---

> *Other Factors.* There are many wild cards unique to particular products, or perhaps simply little used in particular industries, with which you can make your product stand out. For instance, consider a service agreement guarantee. When consumers know they can get a product repaired under a service guarantee or return a faulty product for a refund, they're often more likely to buy it over otherwise superior competitors offering less powerful warranties.

## Cover Your Behind

To a typical consumer who's purchased her share of shoddy products from uncooperative manufacturers, it's encouraging to hear about a multimillion-dollar settlement of a consumer's claim against some manufacturer. It provides proof that the high and mighty can be humbled and that some poor schmuck can be struck by lightning and receive a big fat check.

To manufacturers and distributors of products, however, the picture looks entirely different. Liability lawsuits have changed the landscape of a number of industries, from toy manufacturers to children's furniture retailers. If you visit public swimming pools these days, for instance, you don't see the diving boards that used to grace the deep ends of almost all such recreational facilities. The reason is that fear of lawsuits from injured divers, along with the allied increase in liability insurance premiums, have made these boards no longer financially feasible.

If you're going to come out with a diving board or offer diving board maintenance services, you need to be prepared for this legal issue. Dealing with it may be as simple as merely including a statement to the effect that you foresee no significant liability issues arising from your sale of this product or service. If there is a liability issue, real or apparent, acknowledge it and describe how you will deal with it in your plan. For instance, you may want to take note of the fact that, like all marketers of children's bedroom furniture, you attach warning labels and disclaimers to all your products and also carry a liability insurance policy. In fact, warning labels may seem ridiculous, but in a litigation-crazed society, you will actually see labels such as the one on a portable stroller that read, "Please remove child before folding." Really? Funny as it may sound, let it be known that you will take all necessary steps to protect your business, your products, and yourself from litigation.

You must have an attorney's advice on almost anything you plan to market. A layman's opinion on whether a product is more or less likely to generate lawsuits is not worth including in a plan.

On the subject of liability, here is a good place to deal with the question of whether you are already being sued for a product's perceived failings and, if so, how you plan to deal with it. If you can't find an answer, you may wind up like private aircraft manufacturers, many of which were forced out of the business by increases in lawsuits following crashes.

It's often difficult to get an attorney to commit himself on paper about the prospects for winning or losing a lawsuit. Many times, plans handle this with a sentence saying something along the lines of, "Our legal counsel advises us the plaintiff's claims are without merit."

## What You Need to Know

The following are some key points about products.

▷ *Product knowledge is important, but you need more.* Sure, you have to know the products and services you sell in detail. But product knowledge alone is useless, and that is where many marketing plans run afoul of the first law of marketing: Put the Customer First. Customers don't buy products or services. They buy solutions to problems, relief from an itch, satisfaction of a felt need. In short, they buy benefits.

▷ *Benefits are not features.* Features are characteristics of products or services that are independent of the buyer's perceptions. A tractor lawn mower may have a 3 hp gas motor, be green with a natty yellow design, have a warranty good for two years, and cost $1,695, payable in twelve easy monthly installments. Those are all features.

The benefits to the buyer include confidence (3 hp is plenty powerful for a suburban lawn and will carry its owner in comfort up and down gentle slopes), prestige (John Deere knows how to make its buyers feel good), and convenience and economy (price and terms). Benefits perceived will differ from one customer to the next—another buyer might buy the same lawn mower because his son-in-law is the dealer, or because his neighbor says it's a great machine, or just because it caught his eye.

The key point is that benefits are dependent on the perceptions of the market, whereas features are dependent on the product or service.

▷ *The perceptions of the market are determined only by research.* Armchair research does not count. If you know your market and study your demographics, you will know what your customers perceive to be of value. Then and only then can you safely match your products or services to their demands. You get to know what your markets want by asking them, by knowing them, by researching their buying behaviors. Some of this is almost subliminal—but what sets the big winners apart is that they take the extra time to do this research.

## Chapter 9 Summary

If you are in the wrong industry at the wrong time, making your business grow is going to be difficult. Not impossible, just difficult. The investment community tends to believe that any business can be buoyed by an industry on the rise and that the opposite is true in an industry whose tide is ebbing. This means it's important for you to include an industry analysis in your business plan.

What you'll learn from this chapter:

- How to make yourself an expert in your industry
- How to do research
- What you need to say about trends in your industry
- How to communicate barriers to entry
- How to know who your competitors are
- How to tell readers what makes you better

# Rising Industry Trends

Readers of your business plan may want to see an industry on a fast-growth track with few established competitors and great potential. Or they may be more interested in a big, if somewhat slower-growing, market with competitors who have lost touch with the market, leaving the door open for rivals.

Whatever the facts are, you'll need to support them with a snapshot analysis of the state of your industry and any trends taking place. This can't be mere off-the-cuff thinking. You need to support your opinions with market research that identifies specific competitors and outlines their weaknesses and strengths and any barriers to entry into the market. Finally, and perhaps most important, you'll have to convincingly describe what makes you better and destined to succeed.

> ### Local Is Profitable
> Over 90 percent of all businesses are local. Unless your business is set up to market to regional or larger markets, focus on customers in your immediate geographic location. You can use your knowledge of the conditions and trends in the local economy to your advantage. You can identify and study direct and indirect competitors in the local market far more thoroughly than in a wider area. The better you know your market area, the better you will be able to serve it—and make a profit.

## The State of Your Industry

When preparing the state of the industry section, you'll need to lift your eyes from your own company and your own issues and focus them on the outside world. Instead of looking at your business as a self-contained system, you'll describe the whole industry in which you operate and point to your position in that universe. You can then start to zero in on your country, your state, and your local community, depending on how far your business stretches.

This part of your plan may take a little more legwork than other sections because you'll be drawing together information from a number of outside sources. You may also be reporting on or even conducting your own original research into industry affairs. See Figure 9.1.

> ### ⫸ buzzword
> Psychographics is the attempt to accurately measure lifestyle by classifying customers according to their activities, interests, and opinions. Although not perfect, a psychographic analysis of your marketplace can yield important marketing insights.

## Industry Analysis Questions

To start preparing your industry analysis and outlook, dig up the following facts about your field:

1. What is your total industry-wide sales volume? In dollars? In units?
2. What are the trends in sales volume within your industry?
3. Who are the major players and your key competitors? What are they like?
4. What does it take to compete? What are the barriers to entry?
5. What technological trends affect your industry?
6. What are the main modes of marketing?
7. How does government regulation affect the industry?
8. In what ways are changing consumer tastes affecting your industry?
9. What are recent demographic trends affecting the industry?
10. How sensitive is the industry to seasons and economic cycles?
11. What are key financial measures in your industry (average profit margins, sales commissions, etc.)?

**Figure 9.1.** Industry Analysis Questions

## Market Research

Successful entrepreneurs are renowned for being able to feel a market's pulse intuitively, to project trends before anyone else detects them, and to identify needs that even customers are hardly yet aware of. After you are famous, perhaps you can claim a similar psychic connection to the market. But for now, you'll need to reinforce your claims to market insight by presenting solid research in your plan.

Market research aims to understand the reasons consumers will buy your product. It studies such things as consumer behavior, including how cultural, societal, and personal factors influence that behavior. For instance, market research aiming to understand consumers who buy in-line skates might study the cultural importance of fitness, the societal acceptability of marketing directed toward children and teens, and the effect of personal influences such as age, occupation, and lifestyle in directing a skate purchase.

Market research is further split into two varieties: primary and secondary. Primary research studies customers directly, whereas secondary research studies information that others have gathered about customers. Primary research might be telephone interviews or online polls with randomly selected members of the target group. You can also study your own sales records to gather primary research. Secondary research might come from reports found on the websites of various other organizations or blogs written about the industry.

"When you're starting a business, getting to know your customers is one of the most important things you need to do. If you don't understand your customer, you don't know how you can help solve their problems. You don't know what kind of marketing messages and advertising will work. You don't know if your product or service is actually something your customers will spend money on.

Conducting market research provides answers to those unknown elements. It will greatly reduce risk as you start your business. It will help you understand your competitive position and the strengths and weaknesses of your competitors. And it will improve your marketing and sales process."

(Noah Parsons, "How to Do Market Research — 2023 Guide", Bplans, https://articles.bplans.com/how-to-do-market-research/, 2/3/21)

The basic questions you'll try to answer with your market research include:

 ▷ *Who are your customers?* Describe them in terms of age, occupation, income, lifestyle, educational attainment, and so on.
 ▷ *What do they buy now?* Describe their buying habits relating to your product or service, including how much they buy, their

favored suppliers, the most popular features, and the predominant price points.

⊳ *Why do they buy?* This is the tricky one, attempting as it does to delve into consumers' heads. Answers will depend on the product and its uses. Cookware buyers may buy the products that offer the most effective nonstick surfaces, or those that give the most pans in a package for a given amount of money, or those that come in the most decorative colors.

⊳ *What will make them buy from you?* Although some of these questions may seem difficult, you'd be surprised at the detailed information about markets, sales figures, and consumer buying motivations that is available, especially if you are patient while searching the web. Tapping these information sources to provide the answers to as many questions as you can will make your plan more convincing and your odds of success higher. Also, the business plan software programs have detailed research included and online research available. Utilize this functionality if you are using such software and add additional data you find elsewhere. The reason to add some of your own unique material is that everyone using the software program is tapping into the same database, and you want your business plan to differ from that of the last entrepreneur in your field.

There is also an industry selling market research, and it's a big, booming one. You can find companies that will sell you everything from industry studies to credit reports on individual companies. Market research is not cheap. It requires significant amounts of expertise, manpower, and technology to develop solid research. Large companies routinely spend tens of thousands of dollars researching things they ultimately decide they're not interested in. Smaller firms can't afford to do that too often.

For companies of all sizes, the best market research is the research you do on your own. In-house market research might take the form of original telephone interviews with consumers, customized crunching of numbers from published sources, or perhaps competitive intelligence you've gathered on your rivals through social media. You can gather detailed research on customers, including their likes, dislikes, and preferences through Facebook and use Google Analytics to sort out the numbers as they pertain to your web visitors. People are researching and making their opinions felt through their actions on the web, so you can gain a lot of marketing insight by looking closely at what is going on electronically.

Another likely source of in-house market research is information that comes from data you already have. This information will come from analyzing sales records, gathering warranty cards containing the addresses and other information about purchasers, studying product return rates and customer complaints, and so on. All of this data should be updated and maintained on a regular basis.

You can get in-house market research data from your own files, so it's cheaper than buying it. It's also likely to be a lot fresher than third-party market research, which may be dated or biased.

Of course, if you are starting out, your own customer records will not yet exist, meaning you will need to do your due diligence within your industry. When looking at comparable businesses (and their data), find a close match. For comparative purposes, consider:

1. Companies of relative size.
2. Companies serving the same geographic area, which could be global if you are planning to be a web-based business.
3. Companies with a similar ownership structure. If you are two partners, look for businesses run by a couple of partners rather than an advisory board of twelve.
4. Companies that are relatively new. While you can learn from long-standing businesses, they may be successful today because of their twenty-five-year business history and reputation.

You will want to use the data you have gathered not only to determine how much business you could possibly do but also to figure out how you will fit into and adapt to the marketplace.

One limitation of in-house market information is that it may not include exactly what you're looking for. For instance, if you'd like to consider offering consumers financing for their purchases, it's hard to tell how they'd like it since you don't already offer it. You can get around this limitation by conducting original research—interviewing customers who enter your store, for example, or counting cars that pass the intersection where you plan to open a new location—and combining it with existing data. Follow these steps to spending your market research dollars wisely:

1. Determine what you need to know about your market. The more focused the research, the more valuable it will be.

2. Prioritize the results of the first step. You can't research everything, so concentrate on the information that will give you the best (or quickest) payback.

3. Review less expensive research alternatives. Small Business Development Centers and the Small Business Administration can help you develop customer surveys. Your trade association will have good secondary research. Be creative.

4. Estimate the cost of performing the research yourself. Keep in mind that with the internet you should not have to spend a ton of money. If you're considering hiring a consultant or a researcher, remember this is your dream, these are your goals, and this is your business. Don't pay for what you don't need.

## Talking About Trends

Timing, in business as in other areas of life, is everything. Marc Andreessen, founder of Netscape Communications, had the good fortune to develop software for browsing the web just as the internet, which had been around for twenty years, was coming to widespread popular attention. The timing of his move made him hundreds of millions of dollars, but some browser developers who came later fell by the wayside.

The best time to address a trend is before it is even beginning and certainly before it is widely recognized. If you can prepare a business that satisfies a soon-to-be popular need, you can generate growth that is practically off the scale. (This is, by the way, the combination that venture capitalists favor most.) The problem, of course, is spotting the trends first and acting quickly before others jump in line ahead of you.

There are a couple of different techniques you can use to identify trends and to present your identifications in your plan. A trend is basically a series of occurrences that indicates a pattern. Some trend analysts look at past events (usually trends themselves) and project them forward. For example, trend analysts in recent years have looked at the huge numbers of baby boomers, the surge of people born in the years between 1946 and 1964. They then projected forward to see that these baby boomers would be retiring in the near future and saw a defined market for that segment of the population.

Another good way to forecast trends is by test marketing. You try to sell something in a single store and see how it does before you roll it out in your whole chain. The key to this technique is trying it in a well-selected test market, one that closely resembles the market you'll try to sell to later on.

Focus groups and surveys try to catch hold of trends by asking people what's hot. You can ask open-ended questions: What type of apps or new mobile phone features would you like to see? Or show them product samples and see how they react. This is also tricky because you are dealing with a small group of, you hope, representative people and extrapolating to a larger group. If your group isn't representative, your results may be misleading.

Some other ways you can try to nail a trend in advance: Talk to salespeople who are in touch with customer needs, quiz executives whose jobs are to watch the big picture, read a wide variety of periodicals and try to spot connections, or hire think tanks of experts to brainstorm over what the future might hold.

In most of these trend-forecasting techniques, statistics play a big role. Mathematicians assign numerical values to variables such as loyalty to existing brands, then build a model that can indicate trends that are invisible to intuitive analysis. Providing some statistics in the trends section of your plan can make it more convincing.

## Barriers to Entry

If you want to become a semiconductor manufacturer, you'll need a billion-dollar factory or two. If you want to have a TV network, you'll need programming and cable carriage in the major markets. These problems are called barriers to entry, and they exist to some extent in all industries. The barriers may be monetary, technological, distribution, or market-related, or they may simply be a matter of ownership of prime real estate. (This last is frequently cited as the real competitive advantage of McDonald's.

"Whenever you see a good site, you find out McDonald's already owns it," groused one fast-food competitor.)

An important part of analyzing your market is determining what the barriers to entry are and how high they stretch. If the barriers are high, as is the case with automobile manufacturing, you can be assured new competitors are likely to be slow in springing up. If the barriers are low, such as opening a nail salon, which does not have a huge overhead, you have more opportunity to get into the game.

Be alert for innovative competitors when writing the section of your plan in which you analyze barriers to entry. Clearly some markets are also more saturated than others, and today some are dominated by the McDonald's of their industry. For example, it's hard to open a bookstore today with Amazon changing the way people buy books. In that industry, you need to be creative and explore entry into specialty books, mystery books, or another niche within the larger market. Exploring entry points in the marketplace carefully will save you from a disastrous error and will certainly demonstrate to investors that you've thought your plan through and are not jumping to conclusions.

## Who Are Your Competitors

You're not alone, even if you have a one-person, home-based business. You also have your competition to worry about. And your backers will worry about competition, too. Even if you truly are in the rare position of addressing a brand-new market where no competition exists, most experienced people reading your plan will have questions about companies they suspect may be competitors. For these reasons, you should devote a special section of your plan to identifying competitors.

If you had to name two competitors in the athletic shoe market, you'd quickly come up with Nike and Reebok. But these by far aren't the only competitors in the sneaker business. They're just two of the main ones, and depending on the business you're in, the other ones may be more important. If you sell soccer shoes, for instance, Adidas is a bigger player than either of the two American firms. And smaller firms such as Etonic, New Balance, and Saucony also have niches where they are comparatively powerful.

You can develop a list of competitors by talking to customers and suppliers, checking with industry groups, and reading trade journals. But it's not enough to simply name your competitors. You need to know their manner of operation, how they compete.

---

⟫ **plan pitfall**

Think twice before deciding barriers to entry are high for all potential competitors. For instance, you need billions of dollars to start a semiconductor company—but not if you contract out fabrication of the silicon chips to a manufacturer. Several years back, many semiconductor startups did exactly that, providing serious competition for rivals who assumed the barrier was too high to allow many new entries.

---

Does a competitor stress a selective, low-volume, high-margin business, or does she emphasize sales growth at any cost, taking every job that comes along, whether or not it fits any coherent scheme or offers an attractive profit? Knowing this kind of information about competitors can help you identify their weaknesses as well as their names.

## What Makes You Better?

This is one of the most important sections of your plan. You need to convince anyone thinking of joining with your company, as an investor or in another way, that you offer something obviously different and better than what is already available. Typically, this is called your competitive advantage, but it's not an overstatement to call it your company's reason for being.

"One mistake many new businesses make is thinking that just because nobody else is doing exactly what they're doing, their business is a sure thing. If you're struggling to find competitors, ask yourself these questions.

Is there a good reason why no one else is doing it?

The smart thing to do is ask yourself, "Why isn't anyone else doing it?"

It's possible that nobody's selling cod-liver frozen yogurt in your area because there's simply no market for it. Ask around, talk to people, and do your market research. If you determine that you've got customers out there, you're in good shape.

But that still doesn't mean there's no competition.

How are customers getting their needs met?

There may not be another cod-liver frozen yogurt shop within 500 miles. But maybe an online distributor sells cod-liver oil to do-it-yourselfers who make their own fro-yo at home. Or maybe your potential customers are eating frozen salmon pops right now.

Are there any businesses that are indirect competitors?

Don't think of competition as only other businesses that do exactly what you do. Think about what currently exists on the market that your product would displace.

It's the difference between direct competition and indirect competition. When Henry Ford started successfully mass-producing automobiles in the U.S., he didn't have other automakers to compete with. His competition was horse-and-buggy makers, bicycles, and railroads."

(Tim Berry,"How to Write a Competitive Analysis for Your Business Plan", Bplans, https://www.bplans.com/business-planning/how-to-write/competition/, 4/10/23)

### Chapter 10 Summary

What are you selling? How are you selling it? Why would anybody want to buy from you? Where can they find your product or services? After all, even the greatest invention will not launch a successful business if people do not know where to find it.

Once upon a time the most important aspect of marketing for a brick-and-mortar business was location, location, location—indeed, to a large extent it still is. But today, in the virtual world that is the internet, location may be replaced by Facebook, LinkedIn, Instagram, YouTube, and TikTok.

Your marketing plan is all about knowing your target market and making sure those customers know where they can find you. However, before you can start reaching out to your public, you need to have a marketing strategy that defines what you are selling, at what price(s), from where, and how you are going to spread the word. To simplify, you can use the four Ps of marketing: product, price, place, and promotion.

What you'll learn from this chapter:

- How to define your product and your customer
- Understanding how to set prices in your business
- How to put the product and/or service in a place where people will buy it
- How to promote your business
- How to create a follow-up marketing plan to keep the momentum going

# Marketing: The Plan Within Your Plan

## Defining Your Product

Product, the first of the four Ps, refers to the features and benefits of what you have to sell (as usual, we're using the term as shorthand for products and services). Many modern marketers have a problem with this "P" because it doesn't refer to customer service, which is an important part of the bundle of features and benefits you offer to customers. However, it's pretty easy to update product by simply redefining it to include whatever services are offered.

There are a number of issues you need to address in your product section. You need to first break out the core product from the actual product. What does this mean? The core product is the nominal product. Say you're selling snow cones. A snow cone is your core product. But your actual product includes napkins, an air-conditioned seating area, parking spaces for customers, and so forth. Similarly, an electronics store nominally sells computers, tablets, and devices, but it also provides expert advice from salespeople, a service department for customers, opportunities to comparison shop, software, and so on.

It's important to understand that the core product isn't the end of the story. Sometimes the things added to it are more valuable than the core product itself. That's not necessarily bad, but failing to understand this is likely to lead to trouble.

## Defining Your Customer

Marketing great toys for five-year-olds to teenagers isn't going to work, nor will selling singles cruises to married couples or milkshakes to people who are lactose intolerant. While you may not be able to define everyone who is a likely customer, you need to know your target audience and know it well.

You need to talk about your ideal customer as if he or she is someone you know very well. For example, she or he is twenty-five to twenty-nine years of age, earning $x$ amount of money, has no children yet, and earned a college degree.

A new Italian restaurant might say it's going for families eating out on a budget who live within a five-mile radius of its location. It might quote Census Bureau figures showing there are 12,385 such families in its service area. Even better, it would cite National Restaurant Association statistics about how many families it takes to support a new Italian restaurant.

A bicycle seat manufacturer might have identified its market as casual middle-aged cyclists who find traditional bike seats uncomfortable. It may cite American College of Sports Medicine surveys, saying that sore buttocks due to uncomfortable seats is the chief complaint of recreational bicyclists.

It is important to quantify your market's size if possible. If you can point out that there are more than six million insulin-dependent diabetics in the United States, it will bolster your case for the new easy-to-use injection syringe your company has developed.

In addition to fully defining your product, you need to address other issues in your marketing plan. For instance, you may have to describe the process you're using for product development. Tell how you come up with ideas, screen them, test them, produce prototypes, and so on.

You may need to discuss the life cycle of the product you're selling. This may be crucial in the case of quickly consumed products such as corn chips and in longer-lasting items like household appliances. You can market steadily to corn chip buyers in the hopes they'll purchase from you frequently, but it makes less sense to bombard people with offers on refrigerators when they need one only every ten or twenty years. Understanding the product's life cycle has a powerful effect on your marketing plan, as does knowing logical buying habits. For example, one popular department store was offering a buy-one-get-one-at-half-price deal on fine jewelry. The deal was not generating a strong response because most people do not shop for expensive jewelry in "bulk" quantities but instead take a personalized approach. In fact, such a promotion was cheapening the products.

Other aspects of the product section may include a branding strategy, a plan for follow-up products, or line extensions. Keeping these various angles on products in mind while writing this section will help you describe your product fully and persuasively.

### The Universally Wrong Assumption

It's always easy to market something by saying, "Everyone will love it!" But that's the kiss of death in marketing. No matter how wonderful a product or service may appear, nothing will please "everyone." Therefore, each product or service must have a defined market if you are serious about your business succeeding. Narrow your demographic group by positioning your product appropriately. That may include more than one place, such as bicycles, which might go under "bikes" or "sporting goods," but not "everywhere" or for "everyone."

## Setting Prices

One of the most important decisions you have to make in a business plan is what price to charge for what you're selling. Pricing determines many things, from your profit margin per unit to your overall sales volume. It influences decisions in other areas, such as what level of service you will provide and how much you will spend on marketing. Pricing has to be a process you conduct concurrently with other jobs, including estimating sales volume, determining market trends, and calculating costs. There are two basic methods you can use for selecting a price.

One way is to figure out what it costs you altogether to produce or obtain your product or service, then add in a suitable profit margin. This markup method is easy and straightforward, and assuming you can sell sufficient units at the suggested price, it guarantees a profitable operation. It's widely used by retailers. To use it effectively, you'll need to know all of your costs as well as standard markups applied by others in your industry.

The other way, competitive pricing, is more concerned with the competition and the customer than with your own internal processes. The competitive pricing approach looks at what your rivals in the marketplace charge, plus what customers are likely to be willing to pay, and sets prices accordingly. The second step of this process is tougher—now you have to adjust your own costs to yield a profit. Competitive pricing is effective at maintaining your market appeal and ensuring your enterprise's long life, assuming you can sell your goods at a profit. See Figure 10.1 on page 163 to determine your pricing objectives.

Pricing is inherently strategic. You can use prices to attack competitors, position your business, test a new market, and/or defend a niche. The only hard-and-fast rule to follow in setting prices is: Set prices carefully, deliberately, knowledgeably, and with long-range goals in mind. All the rest are footnotes. See Figure 10.2 on page 164 for help in determining your pricing strategy.

## Setting Pricing Objectives

Before you can select a pricing approach, you need to know your pricing objectives. Following are questions to ask yourself about your pricing goals:

1. Which is more important: higher sales or higher profits?
2. Am I more interested in short-term results or long-term performance?
3. Am I trying to stabilize market prices or discourage price-cutting?
4. Do I want to discourage new competitors or encourage existing ones to get out of the market?
5. Am I trying to quickly establish a market position, or am I willing to build slowly?
6. Do I have other concerns, such as boosting cash flow or recovering product development costs?
7. What will the impact of my price decision be on my image in the market? How does that fit the image I want?
8. What reputation do I want—"sells low and beats prices" or "provides higher-quality goods and/or more personalized service"?

Answer these questions first, then prioritize them to decide how each objective will weigh in setting your pricing strategy. That way, when you present your price objectives in your business plan, it will make sense and be supported by reasonable arguments integrated with your overall business goals.

**Figure 10.1.** Setting Pricing Objectives

# Price Range Worksheet

Pricing is always considered in a competitive context. Part of your pricing strategy involves providing answers to the questions implicit in this worksheet.

Item: Price range: $ _____ (low) to $ _____ (high).

*Establish a price floor*

Mark-on (gross margin) is _____percent of retail price.

Manufacturer's suggested price is $ _____.

Fixed costs are $ _____.

Variable costs are $ _____.

Break-even point is $ _____.

Special considerations for this product or service price:

Level of service:

Status:

Comparative quality:

Loss leader:

Demand:

Product life:

Overhead:

Market penetration costs:

Turnover rate is _____ times per year.

Industry average is $_____.

Going rate is $_____.

I estimate that _____ units will be sold.

Top price (what the market will bear) based on the customers' perceptions of value: $_____.

**Figure 10.2.** Price Range Worksheet

## *Further Pricing Thoughts*

Why is setting price so tough? Perhaps because nobody really understands it. Pricing is as much art as science. Price too low and lose money. Price too high and lose customers. Price in the middle and lose position. It seems like a no-win situation for most small business owners. There is no mechanical way to grind out the right price. There is no shortcut. It's a matter of doing your research, and then it often comes down to some trial and error.

Small businesses simply cannot afford to compete on price. Lowballing drives small businesses out of business, cheapens their image, and costs them the opportunity to upgrade their customer base. It's a race to the bottom and simply does not work.

There's always someone willing to sell on price alone. Sometimes the price competition comes from a giant like Walmart, which buys in such huge quantities that suppliers cave in and pare their margins to the bone. (Walmart has revolutionized inventory management and distribution, which allows them to make vast profits on thin margins. They aren't just competing on price.) Sometimes the competitor is a newcomer who thinks—erroneously—that the best way to enter a market is to buy market share with loss-leader pricing.

The two main ways to deal with price competition are to meet the price (cave in and watch your margins evaporate) or to reposition yourself so the price competition is indirect (repositioning).

## Place

Place refers to channels of distribution, or the means you will use to put your product where people can buy it. This can be very simple: Retailers and many service businesses (restaurants, personal services, business services) rely primarily on location. For manufacturers, conventional distribution systems have three steps: producer, wholesaler, and retailer. You may occupy or sell to members of any one of these steps. Some companies with vertically integrated distribution, such as Apple, occupy all the steps themselves. Others, like franchisors, are parts of systems that orchestrate the activities among all channels. Still others, such as independent retailers, operate in one channel only.

## *Location Considerations*

For retailers, the big place question involves real estate. Location commonly determines success or failure for many retailers. That doesn't necessarily mean the same location will work for all retailers. A low-rent but high-traffic space near low-income housing may be a poor choice for a retailer stocking those Armani suits but will work fine for a fast-food restaurant or convenience store. Your location decision needs to be tied to your market, your product, and your price.

Two of the most common tools for picking location are census data and traffic surveys. Retailers relying on walk-in traffic want to get a location that has a lot of people walking or driving past. You can usually get traffic data from local economic development agencies or by simply sitting down with a clipboard and pencil and counting people or cars yourself. Census data describing the number, income levels, and other information about households in the nearby neighborhoods can be obtained from the same sources. An animal clinic, for example, wants to locate in an area with a lot of pet-owning households. This is the type of information you can get from census surveys. The census website, census.gov, is a great place to start searching for data. You can also learn a lot about marketing research by going to the Insights Association at insightsassociation.org/.

## *Site Sensitivity*

Manufacturers require certain basic conditions for their sites, but retailers and some service firms are exquisitely sensitive to a wide variety of location factors. In some cases, a few feet can make the difference between a location that is viable and one that is not.

Site selection plans for retailers should include traffic data, demographics of nearby populations, estimated sales per square foot, rental rates, and other important economic indicators. Service firms such as restaurants will want many of the same things. Service firms such as pest control services and bookkeeping businesses will want to provide information about local income levels, housing, and business activity.

Store design also must be addressed. Retailing can be as much about entertaining shoppers as it is about displaying goods. So store design becomes very important, especially for high-fashion retailers or well-known tech companies such as Apple. Floor plans are probably not enough here. Retailers may want to include photos or illustrations of striking displays, in-store boutiques, and the like.

Then there is the internet and e-commerce, where physical location gives way to driving traffic to the site. This is where you need a Facebook page, Twitter handle, YouTube channel, Instagram for photos, and so forth. Social media is where e-tailers can make themselves known but only by using the accepted methods of the genre. Social media marketing is a different animal, and that means getting to know your prospective customers online without being sales hungry or pushy. The hard sales push turns off the social media crowd. It is more about engaging effectively and building community.

To get started, however, you need a Facebook page that draws attention and a presence on social media, which can take time to build. Followers on social media serve two very important purposes:

1. They can become regular customers if you keep providing them with products they like to buy.
2. They can spread the word to their social media followers. Word-of-mouth marketing is huge and cost-free to you once you've set the wheels in motion.

The power of the internet is such that it can reach millions of people without your having to pay to reach them. It is light-years ahead of direct mailing, which can work in smaller business circles but does not make sense at a national or global level.

You need to be able to plan a social media campaign, which means adapting to the rules of the road and using any social media platform correctly. It means putting forth your message in a creative and interesting way. This also holds true for blogs. There are tons of bloggers out there, but those who have interesting content get far more readers than those that do not.

In social media, you want to

▷ pose interesting questions
▷ answer the questions of others to demonstrate your expertise

» be transparent and honest

» be consistent and NOT say different things on different platforms

» make friends and build relationships with people rather than selling, selling, selling (social media is "social"; just as you wouldn't start a sales pitch at a party or social engagement, so, too, you wouldn't do it on social media either)

» stay on top of what is going on—don't launch into old news and retreaded themes

» maintain an ongoing presence—participate often and update your web presence

---

**20 Keys to Having an Excellent Website That Enhances Your Marketing Plan**

1.   Update it regularly—nobody wants old news or information.

2.   Use content that interests your visitors—make it about them, not all about you.

3.   Avoid too many bells and whistles that slow down the site.

4.   Make it navigation friendly—people who get lost will leave.

5.   Make it interactive with polls and surveys.

6.   Provide an "about us" page so visitors (including current customers) know who you are.

7.   Use colors that don't glare or make it hard to read.

8.   Check out how the pages look on various computers and mobile devices.

9.   Double-check to make sure all links work.

10.  Maintain control—even if someone else designs it, learn how to make your own changes.

11.  Link only to businesses you know are reliable.

12. Keep it original—you can borrow ideas, but don't use content from other sources, at least not without the permission of the other site owner or manager.

13. Include a blog—if you don't write very well, hire a blogger.

14. Use visuals—photos are worth thousands of words.

15. Link to your social media sites—Facebook, Twitter, LinkedIn, YouTube, Pinterest, and so on. You need not be on all of them—look at their demographics.

16. Make it clear how people can find you if you have brick-and-mortar location(s).

17. Make it clear how they can pay you—and make sure the process is simple—if you are selling on the internet.

18. Include a site map.

19. Use keywords in the site for SEO purposes to be found by search.

20. Have easy-to-find contact information on every page.

### Setting Up Your Online Presence

Every successful business today has at least a website (and some have more than one) as well as a presence on Facebook and other social media sites. Just as you set up a retail store to best position your products, you want to set up your site to do the same. Your social media helps lead customers to your site and your business. It all ties together.

Your website is also influenced by what type of business you are running. For a brick-and-mortar business, it can be an adjunct means of marketing you and your goods.

For a business selling through its locations and on the internet, it is a means of taking local shopping worldwide. Many e-tailers have found that they may carry items that do marginally well in their local stores but have an audience thousands of miles away. That's the beauty of the internet. Of course, this means factoring such shipping into your operations.

For businesses that are strictly web driven, you'll need to show how the site works and all that is set up behind the site for taking orders, shipping them, and handling customer service, which is important for all businesses today, but especially so for online businesses where buyers cannot walk in and return an item face-to-face.

Along with the reasoning behind your site, you'll also want to have a website designed to suit your type of business and demographics. Therefore, a high-end jeweler and kid-friendly fast-food restaurant will look quite different from one another on the web.

You'll also want to keep it simple. Try not to overwhelm the viewers. Some white space isn't a bad thing. It's also important that you have a consistent message (for all marketing). If you're the high-end jeweler, then everything should have the same high-end appeal, photos, and wording. If you're the kid-friendly fast-food place, then everything should be about families and kids. Be consistent.

One of the best ways to determine what you want, whether you end up using site-building software or hire someone to build your site, is to look at other sites and write down what you like.

Many companies devote great time and effort to their web and social media presence. They look at the statistics provided and plan carefully how and when to post their messages.

The more your business is dependent on the internet, the more you will discuss it in your plan of operations. But you should definitely include it in your marketing plans. A business today without any mention of using the internet is suspicious.

### Distribution Concerns

There are three main issues in deciding on a placement strategy: coverage, control, and cost. Cost, it goes almost without saying, is an important part of any business decision, including distribution concerns. The other two issues, however, are unique to distribution and are trickier.

Coverage refers to the need to cover a large or a small market. If you're selling laundry soap, you may feel the need to offer it to virtually every household in America. This will steer you toward a conventional distribution scheme running from your soap factory to a group of wholesalers serving particular regions or industries, to retailers such as grocery stores, and finally to the consumer. It can also be accomplished by selling online, saving you the need for numerous warehouses.

What if you are reaching out to only a small group, such as chief information officers of Fortune 500 companies? In this case, the conventional, rather lengthy distribution scheme is clearly inappropriate. You're likely to do better by selling directly to the CIOs through a company sales staff, sales reps, or perhaps an agreement with another company that already has sales access to the CIOs. In both these cases, coverage has a lot of say in the design of your distribution system.

Control is important for many products. Ever see any Armani suits at Target? The reason you haven't is that Armani works hard to control its distribution, keeping the costly apparel in high-end stores where its lofty prices can be sustained. Armani's need for control means that it deals only with distributors who sell to designer boutiques. Many manufacturers want similar control for reasons of pricing, after-sale service, image, and so forth. If you need control over your distribution, it will powerfully influence placement decisions.

The distribution scheme is of critical importance to manufacturers. Say you make a mass-market consumer good such as a toy. Whether you plan effectively to get your product onto shelves in the major grocery, drug, and discount store chains may make all the difference between success and failure.

If you're selling an informational product to a narrow market, such as political consulting services to candidates for elected office, physical distribution is of less importance. However, for just about all companies, an effective placement strategy is a big determinant of success.

### Scarcity and Urgency Work

One popular approach to marketing is to make products more valuable via scarcity and present a sense of urgency through limited-time offers. From highly touted sales to special sales for preferred customers, a sense of "act now" works in your marketing plans. People also see value in a limited edition or an item that is not always easy to get. Don't make up false scarcity or customers may see through it—but think about what you may run out of and let people know they should order while it's still available. The home shopping channels made a fortune by having a clock ticking away so that people would run to their phones to purchase an item before it disappeared (until tomorrow). Disney offers its classic films for sale through television commercials that ask you to buy now before the film goes back into the vault for years to come.

## Promotion

Promotion is virtually everything you do to bring your company and your product in front of consumers. Promotional activities include picking your company name, going to trade shows, buying advertisements, making telemarketing calls, using billboards, arranging co-op marketing, offering free giveaways, building and maintaining your online presence, and more. Not all promotions are suitable for all products, of course, so your plan should select the ones that will work best for you, explain why they were chosen, and tell how you're going to use them.

Promotion aims to inform, persuade, and remind customers to buy your products. It uses a mix that includes four elements: advertising, personal selling, sales promotion, and publicity or public relations.

### ≫ buzzword

Co-op promotions are arrangements between two businesses to cross-promote their enterprises. When a soft drink can includes a coupon good for a discount on the price of entry to an amusement park, that's a co-op. Countless variations exist.

## *Advertising Concerns*

Advertising is a large part of marketing and promotion for most businesses. In 2022, businesses spent $153 billion on online advertising, or nearly 62 percent of the whole. Television is a distant second with 22.7 percent. Outdoor advertising was third with only 5.2 percent. Print media advertising in newspapers and magazines combined didn't even reach 6 percent. Because most businesses cannot afford television ads, except in local markets, the choices come down to (primarily) print and the internet.

Though the web is the place to be, print still offers some perks. For example, newspapers, magazines, and other forms of print are tangible and stay in people's view somewhere in the house—even on the rare occasion when the computer is turned off. Brand recognition is still easy to spot on the page or on a sign or billboard. Consumers tend to look longer at a print ad and skim less frequently than when they are looking at ads online, and because there are fewer print ads than in the past, your ad can stand out more. Of course. before you can advertise, you need to figure out why you are advertising: What are your goals?

You may be advertising to raise your corporate profile, to improve a tarnished image, or simply to generate foot traffic. Whatever you're after, it's important to set specific goals in terms of such things as revenue increase, unit volume growth for new business, inquiries, and so forth. Without specific objectives, it's hard to tell what you can afford to do and whether the campaign is living up to expectations.

Also, keep in mind that promotional plans, such as giveaways and freebies—caps, pens, T-shirts, and so on—should also be part of your plan to market your business.

---

### ≫ plan of action

You can get mounds of economic and demographic marketing information—much of it free—from the U.S. Census Bureau. To learn more, contact the following office: Economic and Demographic Statistics, Bureau of the Census, U.S. Department of Commerce, Data User Service Division, Customer Service, Washington, DC 20233, www.census.gov, or call (301) 763-4100.

---

### *Other Kinds of Promotion*

Sales promotion is kind of a grab bag of promotional activities that don't fit elsewhere. If you offer free hot dogs to the first 100 people who come to your store on Saturday morning, that's a sales promotion. This category also includes in-store displays, trade shows, off-site demonstrations, and just about anything else that could increase sales and isn't included in the other categories.

Publicity is the darling of small businesses because it lets them get major exposure at minimal cost. If you volunteer to write a gardening column for your local newspaper or a blog for a gardening website, it can generate significant public awareness of your plant nursery and position you as a leading expert in the field, all for the price of a few hours a week spent jotting down some thoughts on a subject you already know very well. To buy comparable exposure might cost thousands of dollars. Press releases announcing favorable news about your company are one tool of publicity; similar releases downplaying bad news, if necessary, are the flip side.

Public relations is a somewhat broader term that refers to the image you present to the public at large, government entities, shareholders, and employees. You may work at public relations through such tools as your website, company newsletters, e-newsletters, legislative lobbying efforts, your annual report, and the like.

Whatever you do, don't neglect public relations and publicity. There is no cheaper or more powerful tool for promotion.

## Follow-Up Plan

Customers may ask, "What have you done for me lately?" Investors and others reading your business plan want to know, "What are you going to do for me tomorrow?" Any serious business plan has to take note of the fact that every product has a life cycle, that pricing pressures change over time, that promotions need to stay fresh, and that new distribution opportunities are opening up all the time. So, the portion of your plan where you describe how you'll continue your success is a vital one.

The annals of business are full of companies that turned out to be one-trick ponies that introduced a product or service that zoomed to stardom but failed to follow it up with another winner. In the best cases, these companies survive but fade back into obscurity. In the worst, they fail to negotiate the switch from booming sales to declining sales and disappear completely.

Diversifying into more than one product is another good way to reduce the risk. It's a good idea to divert part of any boost in revenues to studying market trends and developing new products.

Investors looking at a plan, especially those contemplating long-term involvement, are alert to the risk of backing a one-trick entrepreneur. Showing competitive barriers that you've erected and systems for developing new products is an important part of calming their fears.

There's one caveat when it comes to learning new tricks, however. Very simple concepts are the easiest to communicate, and extremely focused companies usually show the fastest growth—although not always over the long term. So you don't want to appear, in the process of reducing risk, that you've lost sight of the answers to the key questions: What are you selling? How are you selling it? And why would anybody want to buy from you?

### Chapter 11 Summary

The marketing section of your plan addresses a major part of operations: how you identify and attract customers. Operations is concerned with how you buy, build, and prepare your product or service for sale. That covers a lot of ground, including sourcing raw materials, hiring labor, acquiring facilities and equipment, and shipping the finished goods. And it's different ground depending on whether you're a manufacturer, a retailer, or a service firm.

What you'll learn from this chapter:

> » How to describe operations for retail and service businesses
> » How to communicate operations for a manufacturing firm
> » How to understand the impact of information technology on operations

# How Does Your Business Work?

Not surprisingly, investors and other plan readers pay careful attention to the part of your plan describing your operations. Most entrepreneurs are highly expert, interested in operations, and love to talk about it—in fact, one risk is that you'll go into too much detail here and wind up with what amounts to a technical treatise in which the essential marketing element seems lost. David Wheeler recognized that risk when seeking investors for his software startup called InfoGlide Inc. One of his first hires was someone to take on the job of CEO, to interface directly with investors and high-profile prospects so Wheeler could get back to the operations he loved. "That's what I like," he says, "working with database code, not doing product demos."

The basic rule for your operations section is to cover just the major areas—labor, materials, facilities, equipment, and processes—and provide the major details—things that are critical to operations or that give you a competitive advantage. If you do that, you'll answer investors' questions about operations without overwhelming them.

The simplest way to treat operations is to think of it as a linear process that can be broken down into a sequence of tasks. Although several tasks may be performed simultaneously, leave the scheduling to a later part of the operations section. In Figure 11.1, each task is broken down into smaller elements, and as you run your business, you will naturally do so. For your business plan, make sure that the broad outlines of your operations are covered.

Once the initial task listing is complete, turn your attention to who is needed to do which tasks. Keep this very simple. You don't have to look at minor tasks (who opens the door? who fetches the mail?), but you do have to concentrate on major tasks such as producing a product or delivering a service. Use your judgment. Then fill out the form in Figure 11.2 for each major task.

| What Has to Be Done: Task Listing | | | | |
|---|---|---|---|---|
| **Task** | **Daily** | **Weekly** | **Monthly** | **Other (specify)** |
| 1. | | | | |
| 2. | | | | |
| 3. | | | | |
| 4. | | | | |
| 5. | | | | |
| 6. | | | | |
| 7. | | | | |
| 8. | | | | |
| 9. | | | | |
| 10. | | | | |

Figure 11.1. What Has to Be Done: Task Listing

| Tasks Requiring More Than One Person | |
|---|---|
| Name of task | |
| People needed | |
| Elements of the task | |
| Timing (when they do it) | |
| Time allotted | |
| Total time, including support | |
| Comments | |

Figure 11.2. Tasks Requiring More Than One Person

## Operations for Retail and Service Firms

Service firms have different operations requirements from manufacturers. Companies that maintain or repair things, sell consulting, or provide health care or other services generally have higher labor content and lower investments in plants and equipment.

Another important difference is that service and retail firms tend to have much simpler operational plans than manufacturers. In the process of turning raw materials into finished goods, manufacturers may employ sophisticated techniques in a complex series of operations. By comparison, it's pretty simple for a retailer to buy something, ship it to his store, and sell it to a customer who walks in.

That's not to say operations are any less important for retailers and service firms. But most people already understand the basics of processes such as buying and reselling merchandise or giving haircuts or preparing tax returns. So you don't have to do as much explaining as, say, someone who's manufacturing microprocessors.

### *The Importance of People*

For service and retail firms, people are the main engines of production. The cost of providing a service is largely driven by the cost of the labor it entails. And retail employees' skills and service attitudes drive their employers' productivity and market acceptance to a great degree.

A service-firm plan, then, has to devote considerable attention to staffing. Regional educational attainment data will help readers understand why you think you can hire sufficient semi- and high-skilled workers for a service or repair operation. You'll want to include background information and, if possible, describe employment contracts for key employees such as designers, marketing experts, buyers, and the like.

You'll want to walk the reader through the important tasks of these employees at all levels so they can best understand how your business works and what the customer experience is like.

**Service Operations Checklist**
- Staffing completed (or staffing plan completed)
- Organization chart completed
- Marketing implemented
- Sales policies
- Customer relations policies
- Service delivery policies
- Administering monitoring and control policies
- Follow-up procedures

Note that staffing and organizational issues precede marketing, sales, and delivery of the service. Service operations are people-intensive, and careful management goes a long way to making sure that your quality controls are effective.

## Buying

The ability to obtain reliable, timely, and reasonably priced supplies of easily salable merchandise is perhaps the prime skill of any retailer. Buying is both art and science. Knowing what the economical ordering quantities are for a given product is mechanical, but knowing which items to stock requires knowledge of customer desires and demand. Buying is based on your marketing plan. Without clear knowledge of the marketing environment, you cannot make wise purchasing decisions.

### ≫≫ fact or fiction

Is success a matter of buying low or selling high? Retailers say that, contrary to popular opinion, they really make their money when they buy, not sell, goods. The trick, mastered by successful retailers like Walmart and Toys "R" Us, is to buy goods for a price low enough that you can sell them at a profit while still attracting customers and discouraging competitors.

**Retail Operations Checklist**

- Marketing (include sales projections, location, promotional efforts, advertising, and online marketing efforts)
- Staffing
- Training sales staff
- Buying procedures (include delivery times, freight-in, reorder points)
- Inventory control
- In-store sales tools
- Sales policies
- Customer service policies and procedures
- Service delivery policies
- Administering monitoring and control policies
- Follow-up procedures
- Backroom operations staffed

Note the importance of training sales staff and customer service representatives. Many retailers omit this to their economic loss. The major reason consumers give for not returning to a store is discourteous or unhelpful sales staff. Point out that you will train your sales staff so that they will act as a powerful resource for your company.

If you have what consumers want when few of your competitors do, you're almost guaranteed to have strong sales. If you run out of a hot item, on the other hand, disappointed consumers may leave your store, never to return.

Operations plans for retailers, therefore, devote considerable attention to sourcing desirable products. They may describe the background and accomplishments of key buyers. They may detail long-term supply agreements with manufacturers of in-demand branded merchandise. They may even discuss techniques for obtaining, on the gray market, desirable products from manufacturers who try to restrict the flow of goods to their stores.

## Operations for Manufacturers

Companies that make things have certain characteristics in common that set them apart from others, including retailers and service firms. They take raw materials and labor and transform them into sellable products. Although they may also distribute the products and sell direct to customers (thus involving the retail and service aspects of operations), most manufacturers concentrate on the production end and farm out the retail and service to other firms.

### Process Points

The lead actor in manufacturing is the process of production. Product development, marketing, and distribution all play important roles, but it's the production process that sets manufacturers apart from all other enterprises. And the better your production process, the better a manufacturer you will be. It's the star that leads to your company's success.

A manufacturing production process consists of several components. One step is usually fabrication, or the making of products from raw materials. There is also assembly of components, testing, and inspection of finished goods.

Manufacturing processes can become extremely detailed, as is the case with the many parts found in mobile technology. If you're an operations-minded entrepreneur, you may revel in these details. But control your enthusiasm for such detail when it comes to writing a business plan. Stick to the important processes, those essential to your production or that give you a special competitive advantage.

### Personnel and Materials

Manufacturers combine labor and materials to produce products. Problems with either one of these critical inputs spell trouble for your business and for its backers. Business plan readers look for strong systems in place to make sure that personnel and materials are appropriately abundant.

 **plan pointer**

How much detail should you include about the technology you employ? We're living in a highly technical environment. That means you should explain some of the key technology that comes into play during your operations—in lay terms. You need to go into greater detail only if your business relies heavily on technology, sells technology, or utilizes some unique technology that is uncommon in your industry.

**Manufacturing Company Checklist**
- Marketing plan completed
- Staffing completed (or staffing plan completed)
- Organization chart completed
- Product plan completed
- Basic manufacturing operations listed in sequence
- Raw materials purchased
- Equipment obtained
- Labor skills available and assigned
- Timelines and deadlines assigned
- Potential roadblocks identified
- Managerial controls in place
- Sales policies reviewed
- Customer relations policies outlined
- Service delivery policies developed
- Administering monitoring and control policies
- Follow-up procedures checked

Manufacturing is complex. Your checklist will most likely differ from the one given in this sidebar. A small contractor, for example, makes things but is less complex, so might have a checklist like this:

- Develop work schedule
- Hire labor
- Set up equipment
- Acquire necessary materials
- Monitor work schedule

The key point: Identify the major pieces or aspects of your operation in your business plan.

You should show in your plan that you have adequate, reliable sources of supply for the materials you need to build your products. If you are working with suppliers in other parts of the world, show that they are reliable and that you have established a system that will make such international production run smoothly. A global marketplace means that you have more opportunities to find the materials or products you need and to find new markets for sales. This can be impressive to your readers. However, you need to define and provide the details of how your business will benefit from being a part of the global marketplace. Even if you are not planning to actively pursue global partnerships or buy from vendors around the globe or market to customers in other countries, if you are selling via your website, you need to address the possibility of international sales.

Estimate your needs for materials and describe the agreements with suppliers, including their length and terms that you have arranged to fulfill those needs. You may also give the backgrounds of your major suppliers and show that you have backup sources available should problems develop.

It's an interesting spectacle, every now and then, to watch an industrial giant such as an automaker or railroad paralyzed by a labor strike. It illustrates the importance of ensuring a reliable supply of adequately trained people to run your processes. It also illustrates the need for a backup plan.

You'll first need to estimate the number and type of people you will require to run your plan. Startups can do this by looking at competitors' plants or by relying on the founders' prior experience at other companies. Existing firms can extrapolate what they'll need to expand from current operations. Then show that you can reasonably expect to be able to hire what you need. Look at local labor pools, unemployment rates, and wage levels using information from chambers of commerce or similar entities. If you plan to import sizable numbers of workers, check out housing availability, and build an expense for moving costs into your budget.

---

### ⟫ plan pitfall

Stay up on technology if you're in the software industry and be careful. There are numerous ways unscrupulous folks can tap into intellectual property, such as recorded music or films. It is harder than ever to catch those who pirate—or steal—such protected properties. But if you are caught, you can get in real trouble. So be careful not to inadvertently use other people's music, images, and so on. Conversely, protect intellectual properties, and if you see your original material showing up elsewhere, contact an attorney.

---

### The Making of a Baron

The person most famous for building an empire based on ownership of capital equipment is Andrew Carnegie. In the 19th century, this Scottish immigrant to America rose from beginnings as a textile-plant worker to become a baron of steel and oil.

Carnegie was always a hard worker—as a teenage delivery boy he was his family's primary source of income. But it was his savvy in acquiring capital equipment that made him a business legend.

At the age of twenty-one, Carnegie borrowed to buy shares in a new railroad being built near his Pennsylvania home. A few years later, he acquired oil field assets in Titusville, Pennsylvania. In railroad car manufacturing, bridge building, and, finally, iron and steel mills, Carnegie followed the same strategy: Control the means of production.

Shortly after 1900, Carnegie sold out to J.P. Morgan. Those holdings became U.S. Steel.

### Getting Equipped

Manufacturing a product naturally requires equipment. A manufacturer is likely to need all sorts of equipment such as cars, trucks, computers, telecom systems, and, of course, machinery of every description for bending metal, milling wood, forming plastic, or otherwise making a product out of raw materials.

Much of this equipment is very expensive and hard to move or sell once purchased. Naturally, investors are very interested in your plans for purchasing equipment. Many plans devote a separate section to describing the ovens, drill presses, forklifts, printing presses, and other equipment they'll require.

This part of your plan doesn't have to be long, but it does have to be complete. Make a list of every sizable piece of equipment you anticipate needing. Include a description of its features, its functions, and, of course, its cost.

Be ready to defend the need to own the more expensive items. Bankers and other investors are loath to plunk down money for capital equipment that can be resold only for far less than its purchase price. Also consider leasing what you need if you are starting out. Once you show that you are responsible at paying your bills and sales look good, you can apply for a small business loan or a line of credit with greater success.

### The Facilities Section

Everybody has to be somewhere. Unless you're a globe-trotting consultant whose office is his suitcase, your plan will need to describe the facilities in which your business will be housed. Even home-based business owners now describe their home offices, as the trend continues to grow rapidly, thanks largely to mobile communications.

Land and buildings are often the largest capital items on any company's balance sheet. So it makes sense to go into detail about what you have and what you need. Decide first how much space you require in square feet. Don't forget to include room for expansion if you anticipate growth. Now consider the location. You may need to be close to a labor force and materials suppliers. Transportation needs, such as proximity to rail, interstate highways, or airports, can also be important. Next, ask whether there is any specific layout that you need. Draw up a floor plan to see if your factory floor can fit into the space you have in mind. Manufacturers today do most of their ordering and communications online, so you need to make sure that wherever you are located has excellent connectivity.

To figure the cost of facilities, you'll first have to decide whether you will lease or buy space and what your rent or mortgage payments will be for the chosen option. Don't forget to include brokerage fees, moving costs, and the cost of any leasehold improvements you'll need. Finally, take a look at operating costs. Utilities including phone, electric, gas, water, and trash pickup are concerns; also consider such costs as your computer connections, possibly satellite connections, as well as maintenance and general upkeep. See Figure 11.3 on page 189 to analyze your requirements.

## Facilities Worksheet

Use this worksheet to analyze your facilities requirements. Fill out the sections, then test available facilities against your requirements.

*Space Requirements*

Initial space

Expansion space

Total space

*Location Requirements*

Technology requirements including connectivity

Proximity to labor pool

Proximity to suppliers

Transportation availability

*Layout Requirements:*

*Cost Requirements (Dollar Amounts of Estimated Expenses)*

Purchase/lease costs

Brokerage costs

Moving costs

Improvement costs

Operating costs

*Total Cost*

**Figure 11.3.** Facilities Worksheet

These aren't the only operations concerns of manufacturers. You should also consider your need to acquire or protect such valuable operations assets as proprietary processes and patented technologies. For many businesses—Coca-Cola with its secret soft drink formula comes to mind—intellectual property is more valuable than their sizable accumulations of plants and equipment. Investors should be warned if they're going to have to pay to acquire intellectual property. If you already have it, they will be happy to learn they'll be purchasing an interest in a valuable, and protected, technology.

---

>>> **buzzword**

Logistics is the science of moving objects from one location to another. For manufacturers and retailers, the logistics of supplies and products is crucial. For service firms, often the logistics of moving employees around is more important.

---

## Information Technology and Operations

Whatever business you are in, technology most likely plays a key role. Retailers place their orders faster and more accurately using computers and track their inventory while other business owners make international deals thanks to computers and communication technology.

Other key technology that fits into your operations, such as that of a medical equipment manufacturer, should be included in the business plan. Explain how this technology is significant to your business and how it can separate you from your competitors.

## Chapter 12 Summary

Financial data is always at the back of the business plan, but that doesn't mean it's any less important than up-front material such as the description of the business concept and the management team. Astute investors look carefully at the charts, tables, formulas, and spreadsheets in the financial section because they know that this information is like the pulse, respiration rate, and blood pressure in a human being. It shows the condition of the patient. In fact, you'll find many potential investors taking a quick peek at the numbers before reading the plan.

Financial statements come in threes: income statement, balance sheet, and cash flow statement. Taken together they provide an accurate picture of a company's current value, plus its ability to pay its bills today and earn a profit going forward. This information is very important to business plan readers.

You can typically gather information and use an Excel or other financial program to make your spreadsheets. You will also find them available in the business plan software that we discussed at the start of the book. These programs also do the calculations.

What you'll learn from this chapter:

- How to create an income statement
- How to build a balance sheet
- Understanding what your goals and objectives are
- How to lay out a cash flow statement
- How to give your personal financial statement
- Understanding financial ratios
- How to establish solid forecasts

# Show Them the Money

## Income Statement

An income statement shows whether you are making any money. It adds up all your revenue from sales and other sources, subtracts all your costs, and comes up with the net income figure, also known as the bottom line.

Income statements are called various names—profit and loss statement (P&L) and earnings statement are two common alternatives. They can get pretty complicated in their attempt to capture sources of income, such as interest, and expenses, such as depreciation. But the basic idea is pretty simple: If you subtract costs from income, what you have left is profit.

**Keep Spreadsheets Simple**

As a rule, stick with the big three: income, balance sheet, and cash flow statements. These three statements are interlinked, with changes in one necessarily altering the others, but they measure quite different aspects of a company's financial health. It's hard to say that one of these is more important than another. But of the three, the income statement may be the best place to start.

To figure your income statement, you need to gather a bunch of numbers, most of which are easily obtainable. They include your gross revenue, which is made up of sales and any income from interest or sales of assets; your sales, general, and administrative (SG&A) expenses; what you paid out in interest and dividends, if anything; and your corporate tax rate. If you have those, you're ready to go.

You want to leverage your income statement to understand if you're performing better, worse or as expected. This is done by comparing it to your sales and expense forecasts through a review process known as plan vs actuals comparison. You then update projections to match actual performance to better showcase how your business will net out moving forward.

In short, you use your income statement to fuel a greater analysis of the financial standing of your business. It helps you identify any top-level issues or opportunities that you can then dive into with forecast scenarios and by looking at elements of your other financial documentation.

(Noah Parsons, "How to Do a Monthly Income Statement Analysis That Fuels Growth", LivePlan, https://www.liveplan.com/blog/use-profit-and-loss-for-growth/, 7/6/21)

## Sales and Revenue

Revenue is all the income you receive from selling your products or services as well as from other sources such as interest income and sales of assets.

## Gross Sales

Your sales figure is the income you receive from selling your product or service. Gross sales equals total sales minus returns. It doesn't include interest or income from sales of assets.

## Interest and Dividends

Most businesses have a little reserve fund they keep in an interest-bearing bank or money market account. Income from this fund, as well as from any other interest-paying or dividend-paying securities they own, shows up on the income statement just below the sales figure.

## Other Income

If you finally decide that the branch office out on County Line Road isn't ever going to turn a decent profit, and you sell the land, building, and fixtures, the income from that sale will show up on your income statement as "other income." Other income may include sales of unused or obsolete equipment or any income-generating activity that's not part of your main line of business.

## Costs

Costs come in all varieties—that's no secret. You'll record variable costs, such as the cost of goods sold, as well as fixed costs—rent, insurance, maintenance, and so forth. You'll also record costs that are a little trickier, the prime example being depreciation.

---

 **buzzword**

EBIT stands for earnings before interest and taxes. It is an indicator of a company's profitability, calculated as revenue minus expenses, excluding tax and interest.

---

## Cost of Goods Sold

Cost of goods sold, or COGS, includes expenses associated directly with generating the product or service you're selling. If you buy smartphone components and assemble them, your COGS will include the price of the chips, screen, and other parts, as well as the wages of those doing the assembly. You'll also include supervisor salaries and utilities for your factory. If you're a solo professional service provider, on the other hand, your COGS may amount to little more than whatever salary you pay yourself and whatever technology you may use for your business.

## Sales, General, and Administrative Costs

You have some expenses that aren't closely tied to sales volume, including salaries for office personnel, salespeople compensation, rent, insurance, and the like. These are split out from the sales-sensitive COGS figure and included on a separate line.

## Depreciation

Depreciation is one of the most baffling pieces of accounting wizard work. It's a paper loss, a way of subtracting over time the cost of a piece of equipment or a building that lasts many years even though it may get paid for immediately.

Depreciation isn't an expense that involves cash coming out of your pocket. Yet it's a real expense in an accounting sense, and most income statements will have an entry for depreciation coming off the top of pretax earnings. It refers to an ongoing decrease in asset value.

If you have capital items that you are depreciating, such as an office in your home or a large piece of machinery, your accountant will be able to set up a schedule for depreciation. Each year, you'll take a portion of the purchase price of that item off your earnings statement. Although it hurts profits, depreciation can reduce future taxes.

### Interest

Paying the interest on loans is another expense that gets a line all to itself and comes out of earnings just before taxes are subtracted. This line doesn't include payments against principal. Because these payments result in a reduction of liabilities—which we'll talk about in a few pages in connection with your balance sheet—they're not regarded as expenses on the income statement.

### Taxes

The best thing about taxes is that they're figured last, on the profits that are left after every other thing has been taken out. Tax rates vary widely according to where your company is located, how and whether state and local taxes are figured, and your special tax situation. Use previous years as a guidepost for future returns. If you are just opening your business, work carefully with your accountant to set up a system whereby you can pay the necessary taxes at regular intervals.

## Balance Sheet

If the income sheet shows what you're earning, the balance sheet shows what you're worth. A balance sheet can help an investor see that a company owns valuable assets that don't show up on the income statement or that it may be profitable but is heavily in debt. It adds up everything your business owns, subtracts everything the business owes, and shows the difference as the net worth of the business.

Actually, accountants put it differently and, of course, use different names. The things you own are called assets. The things you owe money on are called liabilities. And net worth is referred to as equity.

A balance sheet shows your condition on a given date, usually the end of your fiscal year. Sometimes balance sheets are compared. That is, next to the figures for the end of the most recent year, you place the entries for the end of the prior period. This gives you a snapshot of how and where your financial position has changed.

A balance sheet also places a value on the owner's equity in the business. When you subtract liabilities from assets, what's left is the value of the equity in the business owned by you and any partners. Tracking changes in this number will tell you whether you're getting richer or poorer.

---

### ⫸ plan pitfall

Almost anything can lose value, but for accounting purposes, land doesn't. As a rule, you never depreciate land, although you may depreciate buildings as well as other long-lived purchases.

---

## Assets

An asset is basically anything you own of value. It gets a little more complicated in practice, but that's the working definition.

Assets come in two main varieties: current assets and fixed assets. Current assets are anything that is easily liquidated or turned into cash. They include cash, accounts receivables, inventory, marketable securities, and the like.

Fixed assets include stuff that is harder to turn into cash. Examples are land, buildings, improvements, equipment, furniture, and vehicles.

---

### ⫸ fact or fiction

You always want to maximize profits, right? Savvy entrepreneurs know that managing reported profits can save on taxes. Part of the trick is balancing salaries, dividends, and retained earnings.

---

Tax regulations treat each differently, and you can't exactly do whatever you want. Get good advice and be ready to sacrifice reported profits for real savings.

The fixed asset part of the balance sheet sometimes includes a negative value—that is, a number you subtract from the other fixed asset values. This number is depreciation, and it's an accountant's way of slowly deducting the cost of a long-lived asset such as a building or a piece of machinery from your fixed asset value.

Intellectual properties, such as patents and copyrights, also fall into the asset category. For some companies, a recipe, a formula, or a new invention may actually be their most valuable asset. Of course, the actual value is often very hard to determine. Patents, trademarks, copyrights, exclusive distributorships, protected franchise agreements, and the like do have somewhat more accessible value.

>>> **plan pointer**

The two sides of a balance sheet—assets and liabilities—can be presented side by side or one on top of the other. The first is called columnar format; the second, report format. There's no rule about which is best. Do whatever looks or feels natural.

You'll also have intangibles such as your reputation, your standing in the community, and "goodwill," which are difficult to put a value on. Probably the best way to think of goodwill is like this: If you sell your company, the IRS says the part of the sales price that exceeds the value of the assets is goodwill. As a result of its slipperiness, some planners never include an entry for goodwill, although its value may in fact be substantial.

### Liabilities

Liabilities are the debts your business owes. They come in two classes: short-term and long-term.

Short-term liabilities are also called current liabilities. Any debt that is going to be paid off within twelve months is considered current. That includes accounts payable you owe suppliers, short-term bank loans (shown as notes payable), and accrued liabilities you have built up for such things as wages, taxes, and interest.

Any debt that you won't pay off in a year is long-term. Mortgages and bank loans with more than a one-year term are considered in this class.

---

⫸ **plan pointer**

One of the key characteristics of a balance sheet is that it balances. The bottom lines of both sides of the balance sheet, assets on one half and liabilities on the other, should always equal, or be balanced.

---

## Cash Flow Statement

The cash flow statement monitors the flow of cash over a period of time (a year, a quarter, a month) and shows you how much cash you have on hand at the moment.

The cash flow statement, also called the statement of changes in financial position, probes and analyzes changes that have occurred on the balance sheet. It's different from the income statement, which describes sales and profits but doesn't necessarily tell you where your cash came from or how it's being used.

A cash flow statement consists of two parts. One follows the flow of cash into and out of the company. The other shows how the funds were spent. The two parts are called, respectively, sources of funds and uses of funds. At the bottom is, naturally, the bottom line, called net changes in cash position. It shows whether you improved your cash position and by how much during the period.

"Remember, profits aren't the same as cash.

Profitable companies can run out of cash, and they frequently do because of poor cash flow planning. Here's a very quick explanation of why this occurs.

When your business makes a sale to a customer, but that customer takes 30 or even 60 days to pay their bill, the amount of the sale does show up on the Profit and Loss Statement (also called a P&L or income statement), potentially increasing your profits. But that cash doesn't show up in your bank account until the customer actually pays you. So, your business could make a lot of sales and be profitable, but at the same time be low on cash because customers haven't actually paid for their products or services yet."

(Noah Parsons, "5 Tips for More Accurate and Useful Cash Flow Forecasts", LivePlan, https://www.liveplan.com/blog/3-key-things-watch-youre-forecasting-cash-flow/, 7/19/21)

⟫⟫ **buzzword**

Balance sheets help answer the question, What is the book value of the business? The book value of the business is the net worth (or owner's equity). Most valuation methods for small and midsized businesses use the net worth plus an adjusted earnings or free cash flow multiple to create a rough and ready valuation. If you are just starting out, you will probably feel that you are undervalued because you have nothing on which to base your value. Don't fret: Value grows with time as you build your business. It's better that the value of your business honestly reflects your business. If you recall the dot-com crash of 2000, it was largely the result of many up-and-coming dot-coms being greatly overvalued.

## Sources of Funds

Sources of funds usually has two main sections in it. The first shows cash from sales or other operations. In the cash flow statement, this figure represents all the money you collected from accounts during this period. It may include all the sales you booked during the period, plus some collections on sales that actually closed earlier.

The other category of sources of funds includes interest income, if any, plus the proceeds from any loans, line of credit drawdowns, or capital received from investors during the period. Again, these figures represent money actually received during the period. If you arranged for a $100,000 line of credit but only used $10,000 during this period, your sources of funds would show $10,000.

## Uses of Funds

The sources of funds section often has only a few entries, although some cash statements break out sources of funds by businesses and product lines. But even simple statements show several uses of funds. A cash flow statement will normally show uses such as cost of goods sold; sales, general, and administrative expense (SG&A); and any equipment purchases, interest payments, payments on principal amounts of loans, and dividends or draws taken by the owners.

## Net Change in Cash

Few things feel better for a startup businessperson than having plenty of cash in the bank. And few things offer a better picture of what's going on with cash on hand than the net change in cash line on your business plan. Net change in cash equals the difference between total funds in and total funds out. If you bring in $1 million and send out $900,000, your net change in cash is $100,000. Ideally, you want this number to be positive and, if possible, showing an upward trend.

**fact or fiction**

Is it possible to have too much cash? In fact, it is. If your cash is simply sitting in a bank account, it may be drawing little or no interest. In a typical inflationary environment, it will often lose purchasing power from one day to the next. If you have large amounts of cash and nothing to do with it, consider reinvesting in your company—or perhaps another.

## Other Financial Information

If you're seeking investors for your company, you'll probably need to provide quite a bit more financial information than what is in the income statement, balance sheet, and cash flow statement. For instance, a personal finance statement may be needed if you're guaranteeing loans yourself. Applying business data to other ratios and formulas will yield important information on what your profit margin is and what level of sales it will take for you to reach profitability. Still other figures, such as the various ratios, will help predict whether you'll be able to pay your bills for long. These bits of information are helpful to you as well as to investors, it should be noted. Understanding and, if possible, mastering them will help you run your business more smoothly.

## Personal Financial Statement

Investors and lenders like to see business plans with substantial investments by the entrepreneur or with an entrepreneur who is personally guaranteeing any loans and has the personal financial strength to back those guarantees. Your personal financial statement is where you show plan readers how you stack up financially as an individual.

The personal financial statement comes in two parts. One is similar to a company balance sheet and lists your liabilities and assets. A net worth figure at the bottom, like the net worth figure on a company balance sheet, equals total assets minus total liabilities.

A second statement covers your personal income. It is similar to a company profit and loss statement, listing all your personal expenses, such as rent or mortgage payments, utilities, food, clothing, and entertainment. It also shows your sources of income, including earnings from a job, income from another business you own, child support or alimony, interest and dividends, and the like.

The figure at the bottom is your net income; it equals total income minus total expenses. If you've ever had to fill out a personal financial statement to borrow money for a car loan or home mortgage, you've had experience with a personal financial statement. You should be able to simply update figures from a previous personal financial statement.

Because this is important only to investors or lenders, you want to be careful to include this only when necessary. For a small business looking for a small amount of funding, you may be able to draft something with your accountant verifying your net worth and/or previous year's income.

## Financial Ratios

Everything in business is relative. The numbers for your profits, sales, and net worth need to be compared with other components of your business for them to make sense. For instance, a $1 million net profit sounds great. But what if it took sales of $500 million to achieve those profits? That would be a modest performance indeed.

To help understand the relative significance of your financial numbers, analysts use financial ratios. These ratios compare various elements of your financial reports to see if the relationships between the numbers make sense based on prior experience in your industry.

Some of the common ratios and other calculations analysts perform include your company's break-even point, current ratio, debt-to-equity ratio, return on investment, and return on equity. You may not need to calculate all of these. Depending on your industry, you may also find it useful to calculate various others, such as inventory turnover, a useful figure for many manufacturers and retailers. But ratios are highly useful tools for managing, and most are quick and easy to figure. Becoming familiar with them and presenting the relevant ones in your plan will help you manage your company better and convince investors you are on the right track.

≫≫ plan of action
Wondering how good your credit is? You can get a copy of your credit report from any one of the three major credit bureaus:

- Experian at experian.com
- Equifax at equifax.com
- TransUnion at transunion.com

It is vital for bank loans and other business loans that you are more than aware of your credit score. You should do everything you can to maintain a high score.

## Break-Even Point

One of the most important calculations you can make is figuring your break-even point. This is the point at which revenue equals costs. Another way to figure it is to say it's the level of sales you need to get to for gross margin or gross profit to cover all your fixed expenses. Knowing your break-even point is important because when your sales are over this point, they begin to produce profits. When your sales are under this point, you're still losing money. This information is handy for all kinds of things, from deciding how to price your product or service to figuring whether a new marketing campaign is worth the investment.

The process of figuring your break-even point is called break-even analysis. It may sound complicated, and if you were to watch an accountant figure your break-even point, it would seem like a lot of mumbo-jumbo. Accountants calculate figures with all sorts of arcane-sounding labels, such as variable cost percentage and semi-fixed expenses. These numbers may be strictly accurate, but given all the uncertainty there is with projecting your break-even point, there's some question as to whether extra accuracy is worth all that much.

There is, however, a quicker if somewhat dirtier method of figuring break-even. It is described in Figure 12.1. Although this approach may not be up to accounting-school standards, it is highly useful for entrepreneurs, and more important, it can be done quickly, easily, and frequently as conditions change.

Once you get comfortable with working break-even figures in a simple fashion, you can get more complicated. You may want to figure break-even points for individual products and services. Or you may apply break-even analysis to help you decide whether an advertising campaign is likely to pay any dividends. Perform break-even analyses regularly and often, especially as circumstances change. Hiring more people, changing your product mix, or becoming more efficient all change your break-even point.

---

### ⋙ plan pitfall

Financial reports should be prepared according to Generally Accepted Accounting Principles. GAAP—pronounced "gap"— isn't precise. For instance, you can often choose faster or slower methods of depreciating an asset. Stretching GAAP too far may lead to trouble, such as a shareholder lawsuit. Accountant audits are designed to ensure you don't fall into the gap between GAAP and trouble.

---

## Break-Even Analysis Worksheet

To determine your break-even point, start by collecting these two pieces of information:

1. *Fixed costs.* These are inflexible expenses you'll have to make independently of sales volume. Add up your rent, insurance, administrative expenses, interest, office supply costs, maintenance fees, and so on to get this number. Put your fixed costs here: _____.

2. *Average gross profit margin.* This will be the average estimated gross profit margin, expressed as a percentage, that you generate from sales of your products and services. Put your average gross profit margin here: _____.

Now divide the costs by profit margin, and you have your break-even point. Here's the formula:

**Fixed costs / Profit Margin = Break-even point**

If, for instance, your fixed costs were $10,000 a month and your average gross profit margin 60 percent, the formula would look like this:

**$10,000 / .6 = $16,667**

So in this case, your break-even point is $16,667. When sales are running at $16,667 a month, your gross profits are covering expenses. Fill your own numbers into the following template to figure your break-even point:

$_____ / _____ = $_____.

**Figure 12.1.** Break-Even Analysis Worksheet

### Current Ratio

The current ratio is an important measure of your company's short-term liquidity. It's probably the first ratio anyone looking at your business will compute because it shows the likelihood that you'll be able to make it through the next twelve months.

Figuring your current ratio is simple. You divide current assets by current liabilities. Current assets consist of cash, receivables, inventory, and other assets likely to be sold for cash in a year. Current liabilities consist of bills that will have to be paid before 12 months pass, including short-term notes, trade accounts payable, and the portion of long-term debt due in a year or less. Here's the formula:

**Current assets / Current ratio = Current liabilities**

For example, say you have $50,000 in current assets and $20,000 in current liabilities. Your current ratio would be:

**$50,000 / 2.5 = $20,000**

The current ratio is expressed as a ratio; that is, the example in Figure 12.4 shows a current ratio of 2.5 to 1, or 2.5:1. That's an acceptable current ratio for many businesses. Anything less than 2:1 is likely to raise questions.

 **buzzword**

Liquidity measures your company's ability to convert its noncash assets, such as inventory and accounts receivable, into cash. Essentially, it measures your ability to pay your bills.

**Accounting through the Ages**

If you don't understand accounting as well as you should, you can't blame it on recent innovations. Double-entry accounting dates at least from 1340, and the first book on accounting, by a monk named Luca Pacioli, was published in 1494.

Surprisingly, a medieval accountant would feel quite comfortable with much of what goes on today in an accounting department. But accountants haven't been sitting back and relaxing during the intervening centuries. They've thought up all kinds of ways to measure the health and wealth of businesses (and businesspeople).

There are more ratios, analyses, and calculations than you can shake a green eye shade at. And wary investors are prone to using a wide variety of those tests to make sure they're not investing in something that went out of style around the time Columbus set sail. So, although accounting may not be your favorite subject, it's a good idea to learn what you can. Otherwise, you're likely to be seen as not much more advanced than a fifteenth-century monk.

## Quick Ratio

This ratio has the best name—it's also called the acid-test ratio. The quick ratio is a more conservative version of the current ratio. It works the same way but leaves out inventory and any other current assets that may be a little harder to turn into cash. You'll normally get a lower number with this one than with the current ratio—1:1 is acceptable in many industries.

## Sales/Receivables Ratio

This ratio shows how long it takes you to get the money owed you. It's also called the average collection period and receivables cycle, among other names. Like most of these ratios, there are various ways of calculating your sales/receivables cycle, but the simplest is to divide your average accounts receivable by your annual sales figure and multiply it by 360, which is considered to be the number of days in the year for many business purposes. Like this:

$$\text{Receivables} \times 360 = \text{Sales}$$

If your one-person consulting business had an average of $10,000 in outstanding receivables and was doing about $120,000 a year in sales, here's how you'd calculate your receivables cycle:

$$\$10,000 \times 12 = \$120,000$$

$$1/12 \times 360 = 30$$

If you divide one by twelve on a calculator, you'll get .08333, which gives you the same answer, accounting for rounding. Either way, your average collection period is thirty days. This will tell you how long, on average, you'll have to wait to get the check after sending out your invoice. Receivables will vary by customer, of course. You should also check the receivables cycle number against the terms under which you sell. If you sell on thirty-day terms and your average collection period is forty days, there may be a problem that you need to attend to, such as customer dissatisfaction, poor industry conditions, or simply lax collection efforts on your part.

**buzzword**

Leverage refers to the use of borrowed funds to increase your purchasing power. Used wisely, leverage can boost your profitability. Overused, however, borrowing costs can eradicate operating earnings and produce devastating net losses.

### Inventory Turnover

Retailers and manufacturers need to hold inventory, but they don't want to hold any more than they have to because interest, taxes, obsolescence, and other costs eat up profits relentlessly. To find out how good they are at turning inventory into sales, they look at inventory turnovers.

The inventory-turnover ratio takes the cost of goods sold (better known by the acronym COGS) and divides it by inventory. The COGS figure is a total for a set period, usually a year. The inventory is also an average for the year; it represents what that inventory costs you to obtain, whether by building it or by buying it.

**Average COGS / Average inventory = Inventory turnover**

An example:

**$500,000 / 4 = $125,000**

In this example, the company turns over inventory four times a year. You can divide that number into 360 to find out how many days it takes you to turn over inventory. In this case, it would be every ninety days.

It's hard to say what is considered to be a good inventory-turnover figure. A low figure suggests you may have too much money sitting around in the form of inventory. You may have slow-moving inventory that should be marked down and sold. A high number for inventory turnover is generally better.

### Debt-to-Equity Ratio

This ratio is one that investors will scrutinize carefully. It shows how heavily in debt you are compared with your total assets. It's figured by dividing total debt, both long- and short-term liabilities, by total assets.

**Total debt / Debt-to-equity ratio = Total assets**

Here's a sample calculation:

**$50,000 / 1:2 = $100,000**

You want this number to be low to impress investors, especially lenders. A debt-to-equity ratio of 1:2 would be comforting for most lenders. One way to raise your debt-to-equity ratio is by investing more of your own cash in the venture.

### Profit on Sales

Profit on sales, abbreviated as POS, is your ground-level profitability indicator. Take your net profit before taxes figure and divide it by sales.

**Profit / Sales = Profit on Sales**

For example, if your restaurant earned $100,000 last year on sales of $750,000, this is how your POS calculation would look:

**$100,000 / $750,000 = 0.133**

Is 0.133 good? That depends. Like most of these ratios, a good number in one industry may be lousy in another. You need to compare POS figures for other restaurants to see how you did.

### Return on Equity

Return on equity, often abbreviated as ROE, shows you how much you're getting out of the company as its owner. You figure it by dividing net profit from your income statement by the owner's equity figure—the net worth figure if you're the only owner—from your balance sheet.

**Net profit / Net worth = Return on equity**

## Return on Investment

Your investors are interested in the return on investment, or ROI, that your company generates. This number, figured by dividing net profit by total assets, shows how much profit the company is returning based on the total investment in it.

**Net profit  /  Total assets  =  Return on investment**

For example, it might look like this:

**$2,589  / $47,017  =  5.5%**

# Forecasts

Business plans and financing proposals are based on projections. Past financial data can only support your projections, However, financial projections in your business plan express in common financial terms and formats how you expect the immediate future to play out the scenarios you created in the body of the plan. You can forecast financial statements such as balance sheets, income statements, and cash flow statements to project where you'll be at some point in the future.

Forecasts are necessities for startups, which have no past history to report on. Existing businesses find them useful for planning purposes. Forecasts help firms foresee trouble, such as a cash flow shortfall, that is likely to occur several months down the road, as well as give them benchmarks to which they can compare actual performance.

It's always advisable to be somewhat conservative in your forecasts.

> "You need to revisit and update your forecasts. If your budget and forecasts from the beginning of the fiscal year are static and unchanging, it's hard to see how the changes you're planning on making will impact your business financially. It's also hard to communicate the changes you're planning to make to the rest of your team.

Static budgets don't adjust to new situations and in fact, they become more and more outdated as the year goes on. What may have been small variances at the beginning of the year can become larger and larger as actual results naturally differ.

Once a budget is stale and outdated, it's easy to ignore because it doesn't reflect the current situation your business is in. And especially during a crisis, when things can fluctuate rapidly, you don't want budgets and forecasts that you just ignore. Having them up to date can mean the difference between survival and growth, or mismanagement and dwindling performance."

(Noah Parsons, "How to Better Manage Your Business by Creating a Live Forecast", LivePlan, https://www.liveplan.com/blog/live-forecast-method/, 4/16/21)

## EVA Sigh of Relief

EVA is an acronym standing for economic value added, and it's one of the most interesting financial management tools available to business owners. The aim of EVA is to find out whether you're doing better with the money you have than you could by, say, investing in U.S. Treasury bills.

EVA has been pioneered by consulting firm Stern Stewart, which has counseled hundreds of companies on how to apply EVA. And experts say that entrepreneurs in particular already understand EVA on a gut level. In any event, the basic concept is fairly simple—you measure EVA by taking net operating earnings before taxes and subtracting a reasonable cost of capital, say 12 percent.

> In practice, however, it's complicated. Stern Stewart has identified more than 160 adjustments a company may potentially need to make to accounting procedures before EVA can be effectively implemented. Check them out at sternstewart.com.

### Projected Income Statement

Business planning starts with sales projections. No sales, no business. It's that simple. Even if you're in a long-range development project that won't produce a marketable product for years, you have to be able to look ahead and figure out how much you'll be able to sell before you can do any planning that makes sense.

Now that the pressure's on, making a sales projection and the associated income projection may look a little tricky. So let's do it step-by-step.

First pick a period for which you want to make a projection. You should start with a projection for the first year. To do so, you want to come up with some baseline figures. If you're an existing business, look at last year's sales and the sales of prior years. What's the trend? You may then be able to simply project out the 10 percent annual sales increase that you've averaged the past three years for the next three years.

If you're a startup and don't have any prior years' figures to look at, look for statistics about other businesses within your industry. The most important question to ask is: What has been the experience of similar companies? If you know that car dealers across the nation have averaged 12 percent annual sales gains, that's a good starting point for figuring your company's projections.

"When you're forecasting your sales, the first thing you should do is figure out what you should create a forecast for. You don't want want to be too generic and just forecast sales for your entire company. On the other hand, you don't want to create a forecast for every individual product or service that you sell.

For example, if you're starting a restaurant, you don't want to create forecasts for each item on the menu. Instead, you should focus on broader categories like lunch, dinner, and drinks. If you're starting a clothing shop, forecast the key categories of clothing that you sell, like outerwear, casual wear, and so on.

You'll probably want between three to ten categories covering the types of sales that you do. More than ten is going to be a lot of work to forecast and fewer than three probably means that you haven't divided things up quite enough.

You really can't get this wrong. After all, it's just forecasting and you can always come back and adjust your categories later. Just pick a few to get started and move on."

(Noah Parsons, "How to Do a Sales Forecast for Your Business the Right Way", LivePlan, https://www.liveplan.com/blog/the-best-way-to-forecast-sales-and-revenue/, 6/8/21)

≫ **plan pointer**

There are four kinds of financial ratios: liquidity ratios like the current ratio, asset management ratios like the sales/receivable cycle, debt management ratios like the debt-to-equity ratio, and profitability ratios like return on investment.

You'll also need to do your due diligence to get an idea of how much volume you can expect and what factors will have a positive or negative impact upon your ability to sell.

For example, how many people can your restaurant expect to serve in a given day? Statistics of other restaurants may be hard to find, so you may have to do some research by simply watching customers enter and leave a similar type of restaurant for a couple of days during the breakfast, lunch, and dinner hours. Once you get a feel for how many people it is drawing on average, you can begin to estimate how many you may draw. Take into consideration your location vs. its location and the fact that it has regular customers who are familiar with the menu.

Statistics you can look at include how many people are within a few miles and what percentage meet your demographics. For example, a family-friendly restaurant wants to know how many families are living nearby, while a fine-dining establishment wants to get statistics on how many people with a higher income are living within a few miles of the establishment.

For retailers, the difficult part is determining how much market share you can expect. You need to factor in the need for your product in a given community, which can range from local neighborhoods to worldwide if you are selling on the web. Volume will be the toughest thing to estimate. Try to remain conservative in your estimates, knowing that you may not be selling a lot of products or services right off the bat.

Forecasting expenses is your next step, and it's much easier. You can often take your prior year's cost of goods sold, adjust it either up or down based on trends in costs, and go with that. The same goes for rent, wages, and other expenses. Even startups can often find good numbers on which to forecast expenses because they can just go to the suppliers they plan to deal with and ask for current price quotes plus anticipated price increases.

### Projected Balance Sheet

Balance sheets can also be projected into the future, and the projections can serve as targets to aim for or benchmarks to compare against actual results. Balance sheets are affected by sales, too. If your accounts receivables go up or inventory increases, your balance sheet reflects this. And, of course, increases in cash show up on the balance sheet. So it's important to look ahead to see how your balance sheet will appear given your sales forecast.

When you sit down to prepare a projected balance sheet, it will be helpful to take a look at past years' balance sheets and figure out the relationship of certain assets and liabilities that vary according to sales. These include cash, receivables, inventory, payables, and tax liabilities.

If you have any operating history, you can calculate the average percentages of sales for each of these figures for the past few years and use that for your balance sheet projection. You can simply take last year's figures if you don't think they'll change that much. Or you can adjust the percentage to fit some special knowledge you have about the coming year—you're changing your credit terms, for instance, so you expect receivables to shrink, or you're taking out a loan for an expensive new piece of equipment. Firms without operating history can look at one of the books describing industry norms referred to earlier to get guidance about what's typical for their type of company.

### Cash Flow Pro Forma

Businesses are very sensitive to cash. Even if your operation is profitable and you have plenty of capital assets, you can go broke if you run out of cash and can't pay your taxes, wages, rent, utilities, and other essentials. Similarly, a strong flow of cash covers up a multitude of other sins, including a short-term lack of profitability. A cash flow pro forma (or cash budget) is your attempt to spot future cash shortfalls in time to take action.

---

》》》 **plan pitfall**

Pro forma and projected financial statements are based on the future and, as such, are imprecise. You need to make them as realistic and reasonable as possible but not believe in them too explicitly. Be extra sure not to overstate revenue or understate expenses.

---

A cash budget differs from a cash flow statement in that it's generally broken down into periods of less than a year. This is especially true during startup, when the company is sensitive to cash shortages and management is still fine-tuning its controls. Startups, highly seasonal businesses, and others whose sales may fluctuate widely should do monthly cash flow projections for a year ahead, or even two. Any business would do well to project quarterly cash flow for three years ahead.

>>> **plan pointer**

When making forecasts, it's useful to change dollar amounts into percentages. So if you figure sales will rise 20 percent next year, you'll enter 120 percent on the top line of the projection. Using percentages helps highlight overly optimistic sales projections and suggests areas, especially in costs, for improvement.

**The Most Important Financial Statement**

If you have only one financial statement to manage your business by—and to use in your business plan—let it be the cash flow pro forma. Only the cash flow pro forma can tell you how much capital you will need in a startup (add the startup costs, project the cash flow, then make the cash flow positive by providing capital in the indicated amount). Only the cash flow pro forma will tell you when you will need to borrow money— and how much you will need to borrow. Only the cash flow pro forma will tell you when it is time to pull the plug and bail out before you create negative value in your business.

Used as a budget, your cash flow pro forma will keep you from making spontaneous purchases, help evaluate the cost (in cash flow) of growth, hiring new people, adding facilities or equipment, or taking on more debt.

No business can prosper without a cash flow pro forma.

The added detail makes monthly cash flow forecasts somewhat more complicated than figuring annual cash flow because revenues and expenses should be recorded when cash actually changes hands. Sales and cost of goods sold should be allotted to the months in which they can be expected to actually occur. Other variable expenses can be allocated as percentages of sales for the month. Expenses paid other than monthly, such as insurance and estimated taxes, are recorded when they occur.

As with the balance sheet projection, one way to project cash flow is to figure out what percentage of sales historically occurs in each month. Then you can use your overall sales forecast for the year to generate monthly estimates. If you don't have prior history, you'll need to produce estimates of such things as profit margins, expenses, and financing activities using your best guesses of how things will turn out.

The cash flow pro forma also takes into account sources of cash other than sales, such as proceeds from loans and investments by owners.

### Finding Free Cash Flow Apps

They say there's an app for everything. You can now find cash flow projection templates in popular business applications. They may not be highly sophisticated, but they do provide the templates for several key spreadsheets. Google Docs, Intuit's QuickBooks, Pulse, and PlanGuru are among the places to look for cash flow templates. They can make setting it all up a lot easier.

## Positive Cash Flow = Survival

Some key points about cash flow:

Cash flow buys time (if necessary), builds assets and profits, and keeps suppliers, bankers, creditors, and investors smiling. Without positive cash flow, survival becomes questionable. Negative or feebly positive cash flow is painful, and unless corrected will either kill a business or damage it so seriously that it never lives up to its potential. Although short periods of negative cash flow occur in almost every business, cash flows have to be positive at least on an annual basis. Some farmers do very well indeed with cash flows that are strongly negative for eleven months of the year. So do some manufacturers (especially in the garment trade). The key is that they know what their cash flow patterns are—and take steps to finance the negative periods, offsetting that cost against the occasional strong positive cash influx from operations.

Unfortunately, the smaller and more thinly capitalized the company, the less able it is to survive extended negative cash flows. This is one reason why so many startups fail. The business idea may be terrific, but sales always come much more slowly than expected while cash goes out twice as fast. And the initial investment is rarely enough to tide the business along until cash flow turns and stays positive.

How can a small business attain positive cash flow? Discipline. A cash flow budget is an unbeatable tool if followed carefully. If there is to be just one financial statement, make sure it's the cash flow pro forma. It acts at once as a cash flow budget and as a benchmark for sales.

Some people have trouble differentiating the cash flow pro forma from the projected P&L. The concept "profit" is so pervasive that it poses a barrier to understanding that positive cash flow does not equal profit (or vice versa). The example of a profitable growing company with negative cash flow succumbing to illiquidity and tumbling into Chapter 11 bankruptcy is commonly cited to disprove the identity. If the sales don't turn to cash soon enough, the company goes broke. Revenues are up, receivables are up, expenses are up, even profits are up. Yet the company runs out of cash, can't pay its bills, and becomes another cash flow victim.

Another conceptual problem is equating P&L losses with negative cash flow. A loss on the P&L can reflect a negative cash flow, but it doesn't have to. For example, publishing companies enjoy some accounting foibles such as deferred income (which suppresses sales by deferring revenues to a later period). The cash comes in December, but because the revenue is not earned until the following year, the company can show a nice loss for tax purposes, while enjoying strongly positive cash flow.

Some ways to understand cash flow (as distinct from P&L categories) include:

> ⟫ *Students are adept at managing skinny cash flows.* They postpone bill paying, share space to lower costs, use secondhand books whenever possible (if they have to pay the bill, that is), minimize food costs, and so forth. Few of them think of this as cash flow management, but it is—and of a very high order. If they want a ticket to a concert or

ball game, they find a way to scrape up the cash. Very few companies are as carefully managed.

⟩ *Emphasize timing.* Timing is everything for cash flow—the transfers of cash, even the dates that bills fall due or when discounts can or cannot be taken. Although timing is always important in business, it is especially important in managing cash flow. A P&L can stand a bit of looseness—it doesn't matter whether a bill is received January 31 or February 10. That ten days can make a big difference in cash flow if the bill falls due before you have the cash in hand to pay it.

⟩ *Compare cash flow to a checking account.* Cash is deposited (cash inflow). Checks are written (cash outflow). The aim is to always have some cash on hand (positive cash flow).

The cash flow pro forma is the most important single financial statement in the business plan. Every business needs an annotated cash flow pro forma (by month for the first year, by quarter thereafter) reflecting its business idea.

# Turn On the Lights

## *Section Summary*

Now the frame and the materials in your business plan are ready for people to explore. But you have to introduce your readers to your plan and what it's about, and in this section, we start by talking about what goes into your cover letter in Chapter 13. If you need help with creating a business plan and supporting your business, we conclude this section by giving you plenty of resources in Chapter 14.

### *Chapter 13 Summary*

It does not matter how compelling your story is if the reader starts with a negative impression. A shopworn plan reeks of failure from the get-go. Make sure that the cosmetics are right: clean paper, crisp font, clear pictures, and a professional presentation go a long way toward securing a fair reading or hearing of your business plan.

As always, keep your audience in mind. Businesslike is almost always best as a fallback decision on how to make a good first impression.

Ask, in advance, if the recipient wants a hard copy or an e-copy of your plan. In the digital age, we want to give people what they want.

What you'll learn from this chapter:

- How to write an effective letter of introduction
- How to create cover letters and cover sheets

# You Only Make a First Impression Once

## Letter of Introduction

A letter of introduction should be emailed (or mailed) to whomever you would like to read your business plan. In the current business world, sending unsolicited, unanticipated business plans with a mere cover letter will typically not get your plan read. Not only are most people too busy to read whatever comes across their desk or lands in their inbox, they also do not want to be sued someday for "stealing your ideas," even if they never read your plan.

Your letter of introduction is your way of asking them if they would be interested in reading your business plan. Within

225

the letter you explain why you have selected them and what you have to offer, in a brief, compelling manner.

You should also explain generally what you're looking for—an investor, a loan, a long-term supplier relationship, or something else. Often this will be obvious from the circumstances. The introductory letter provides a valuable forum for you to explain why you're contacting this particular person. If you've received a personal referral, you'll want to include who gave you the referral very early on, probably in the first sentence following the salutation. Never underestimate the power of a personal referral from a friend, colleague, or acquaintance. It may not land you an investor, but it gets your foot in the door. When emailing the individual, you might put the referral in the subject line. However, don't send a plan without a letter of inquiry first.

NOTE: Some investors (VCs or even angels) do request plans on their websites. Read the website and make sure you follow its guidelines. For example, if it says send a plan of no more than twenty pages, do not send a forty-two-page plan.

In a world of "who you know" and networking, many of the people you will be sending to are referred by others. In some cases, you may even have some personal connection to the person other than a referral. For instance, perhaps you once met this individual while networking. Perhaps you even worked together at a company or organization. A shared interest, such as a hobby, is of less value, but it may be worth mentioning if your shared interest is unusual or marked by a close degree of identification among those who share it. For instance, it may not mean much to point out that you, like the reader, are a fan of professional basketball. In fact, it may sound a little like you are grasping at straws to make a connection. However, if you both have competed as crew members on long-distance ocean-racing sailboats, this might be worth mentioning. In any case, the cover letter, not the plan, is obviously the place to bring up this type of personal connection.

Finally, the letter of introduction may detail the terms under which you are presenting your plan. You may, for instance, say that you are not submitting the plan to any other investor. You may explicitly point out that you are currently seeking financing from a number of sources, including this one. If there is a deadline for responding to your plan, if you wish to stress that the plan is confidential and must be returned to you, or if you would like to ask the recipient to pass it on to someone else who may be interested, this is the place to do so. Somewhere between sending the introductory letter and sending the plan—if the person agrees to see it—is where you can email a nondisclosure agreement if you plan to include one.

The letter of introduction gives you a chance to provide updated, expanded, or other important information that isn't in your plan. But mostly, it is a letter of introduction and designed to whet their appetite.

## Cover Letters and Cover Sheets

A cover letter is a brief letter stating that you are including the business plan that the recipient has acknowledged and asked you to send over after reading your letter of introduction. It goes in the email that includes the plan or on top of a hard copy, and thanks the recipient for agreeing to take a look at the plan. It is a thank-you—basically a brief note to accompany the plan and thank them for taking a look.

The first thing anyone looking at your business plan will see is the cover page. After that, they may never look at it again.

A few cover page components are essential, whether you are using an email or sending a hard copy. You should definitely have your company name, address, phone number, email address, Twitter handle, and other contact information. Other good items to include are the date as well as a notice that this is, indeed, a business plan. Format this information in a large, black, easily readable font. You want, above all else, for a plan reader to know which business this plan is for and how to contact you.

If you have a striking, well-designed corporate logo, it's also a good idea to include that on the cover page. A corporate slogan, as long as it's not too long, is also a good identifying mark that does something to communicate your strategy as well.

It's tempting to put all kinds of stuff on the cover page, but you should probably resist it. Your business concept, the amount you're trying to raise, and other details can go on the inside. The cover page must identify the company. More than that is likely to be too much.

> *"If you have a striking, well-designed corporate logo, it's also a good idea to include that on the cover page to show that you've put thought into how you present your business to the world."*

## Helpful Layout Tips

Formatting your plan is easy in Microsoft Word and easier in business software. The key is that everything has its own section, is easy to read, and does not look cluttered. You also want to check that you can read the plan on various mobile devices, so test it by checking it out on your iPhone or any other device available.

Keep colors to a minimum and look at photos to see how they appear on other devices and other operating systems.

White space on a page is not your enemy.

Use 1.5 or double spacing. Keep the background white and use black type. Convert the document into a PDF file, with Adobe Acrobat, and keep the file in one document. Include a table of contents, and make sure to check that what you have in there shows up on the specified pages. Also try to align headings so that they do not start at the bottom of a page. You can use tabs for addendums or a separate document for the additional materials such as an appendix.

Also make sure any graphics are clear and do not take too long to load.

 **fact or fiction**

If a plan is used for internal purposes only, it doesn't matter what it looks like as long as it's functional, right? That's true to some extent, but it's also true that part of a plan's functionality is to convince and persuade. A plan that looks shabby and casually thrown together won't command as much respect among other managers and employees as one that's polished and professional looking.

### Hard Copies

Yes, you may still be asked for a hard copy, so be ready to send one. Use good-quality white paper, then bind pages together permanently into a booklet. Any copy shop or printer can do such a binding for you, or you may purchase a do-it-yourself binding kit at an office supply store. Cover your plan with a clear plastic binder so that the cover page shows or print your cover page information on a heavy piece of paper to serve as a cover for the binder.

Permanent binding helps plan readers keep all the pages of your plan together and makes it easier to read. It's important to keep these reasons for permanent binding in mind—it's a decision that improves the functionality of the plan, not its looks. Spending a lot of money creating a beautiful, perfectly bound plan is not a wise investment. Plan readers are interested in information, not entertainment.

The same thing goes for choosing the paper and typeface you'll use in your plan. Pick white paper, or at most perhaps gray, cream, or some shade of off-white, but leave the colored paper to flyers from the pizza place down the street. To make a businesslike impression, use businesslike stationery.

---

⟫⟫⟫ **plan pointer**

Use as many charts, tables, and other graphic elements as it takes to get your point across. But don't count on lavish visuals to sway a skeptical reader. Some readers actually are put off by plans that seem to be trying to wow them through the presentation.

---

### Presenting—Your Business Plan!

Once you've prepared your plan for presentation, put it in front of the right people. There are six steps:

1.  *Obtain leads and referrals.* Find names, addresses, and telephone numbers of investors of the type you wish to target. Ask people you know for referrals. Network as much as possible.

2. *Research your target.* Learn as much as possible about how much money people have to invest, industries they're interested in, and other requirements. Search venture capital directories, Who's Who publications, news articles, websites, and similar sources.

3. *Make your pitch.* First, email or mail an introductory letter to your target letting him know you have a plan you would like to send. If you do send an email or a letter asking him to read your plan and do not hear from him within a short time, send a follow-up email in a week, and try once more about two weeks later (in case he was out of town or swamped with other work). If this doesn't produce a meeting, look elsewhere. We'll talk more about pitching your plan in ten minutes later in this chapter.

4. *Try to meet people in person.* Despite the fact that we are living in a text, email, and conference-call age, you should still try to meet your recipient face-to-face, especially if you are seeking any type of funding. It's very hard to get such a commitment through a few texts or by email. Skype may work, but meeting in person for a major financial commitment is best. Nonetheless, if they want to keep all communication electronic, then follow their lead.

5. *Defuse objections.* Although you may think you've answered everything in your plan, you haven't. Prepare a list of possible objections—potential competitors, hard-to-buttress assumptions, and the like—that your investor may raise. Then prepare cogent answers. Have friends, coworkers, and your team play devil's advocate and provide every possible objection or tough question— then formulate your answers.

6. *Get a commitment.* You won't get an investment unless you ask for it. When all objections have been answered, be ready to offer one last concession—"If I give your representative a board seat, can we do this today?"—and go for the close.

### Pitching Your Business Plan in 10 Minutes

Delivering a good pitch for your business is as much about conveying emotion as conveying information. The saying "They don't care what you know until they know that you care" is good advice to follow.

A pitch doesn't need to be long, and your audience will appreciate it if you keep the pitch as brief as possible. With that in mind, you can put together a pitch in ten minutes that's broken down into one topic every minute.

- ⟩ *Minute 1: Personal introduction.* Let the audience know that you personally care about the people and the problem you are trying to solve.
- ⟩ *Minute 2: State the problem.* People with this problem have emotions invested. They may be struggling, irritated, angry, and/ or disenfranchised. Keep human emotions real. Break down the problem into its component parts accompanied by a diagram.
- ⟩ *Minute 3: Present the solution.* Show excitement and passion for your business's solution. Walk the audience not only through how the solution works, but also through the great benefits of the solution.
- ⟩ *Minute 4: Show your business model.* Now is the time to tell the audience how you will make money. Explain how you are going to charge people for the solution you are offering.
- ⟩ *Minute 5: Talk about your competition.* Do not talk about how you're better than the competition. Instead, focus on how you're different. Your attitude toward the competition gives the audience a peek into your business soul. Are you dutifully respectful of their presence and power or are you arrogant enough to think your little startup will have no problem beating them? Err on the side of humility.
- ⟩ *Minute 6: Talk about your market and how you'll sell to them.* Get excited as you talk about how many potential customers are out there and how you're going to get them. Take the audience through the market data, your chosen point of entry, and your sales and marketing strategy.
- ⟩ *Minute 7: Tell the audience about how much money you'll make.* Talk about how selling to your market shows the unit economics of a single customer (price), and the size of the market shows how many potential deals are out there (quantity). Armed with this information, you can describe how revenue builds over time.

▷ *Minute 8: Introduce your team.* It's important to introduce your team in the context of the business so the audience understands why it is what it is. If you introduce the team up front, you will have to circle back to describe their roles later, which wastes time.

▷ *Minute 9: Prove your business has traction.* You need to show results to get investors and customers to buy in. So, answer important questions such as: What has the team accomplished? Does the company have revenue? Are the customers happy?

▷ *Minute 10: Ask for the buy-in.* You need to spend the last minute asking for people to buy into your business and your vision, no matter if that's asking investors for money or asking someone to work for you. In this last minute, paint a clear picture of what you need from the audience and what investing with you will look like.

### *Be Flexible*

If there is a problem with your plan, you want to know about it. If the projected return to investors is so low that nobody is going to take you seriously, now's the time to find out, not after you've presented it unsuccessfully dozens of times.

So gently probe, asking questions that focus on your plan, to find out whether you've made a mistake or just hit an unreceptive audience. If you identify a failing, of course, fix it before submitting your plan to another party.

Also, be ready to compromise. Perhaps they will give you 50 percent of what you are seeking in funding until they see some results. Consider the offer. You can always go for more funding elsewhere or scale down the size of your endeavor for the time being.

### *Get a Referral*

Even a total refusal to consider your plan is helpful if the person suggests another place where you might be successful. You should always ask for a referral from anyone who turns your proposal down. It can't hurt—you've already been nixed. And a referral from a knowledgeable, respected investor can carry a lot of weight when you use it as an introduction (even if he or she is just trying to get rid of you).

Venture investing is very much a network-driven business. Venture capitalists are always asking for referrals, and they're usually willing to give them as well. Often, they know someone else who might be interested. The same goes for angel investors.

## Keep the Door Open

If an investor doesn't respond to your plan, brushes you off, or even rudely tells you to get lost, your response should still be unfailingly courteous and professional. If you let your frustration, disappointment, hurt feelings, and anger show, it could cost you plenty. That investor may be having a bad day and change her mind tomorrow. She may recall your name and the way you behaved so well under pressure and mention it to a more open-minded associate the next week. Or perhaps next year, when you're promoting a more exciting concept, she'll be willing to back the improved idea.

None of these scenarios is certain or even probable in any individual instance. But considering the aggregate potential to help or hurt you that all the people you'll present your plan to will possess, any of these scenarios is quite likely. And they're only possible if you keep the door open for the future.

### Chapter 14 Summary

Much of the business planning process involves research and communication—research about your product, its market, financial resources, your customers, and your competition along with communication with others in your line of work: industry experts, suppliers, and prospective customers. That's why the internet is an invaluable tool for small business owners. Whether you're writing a business plan for a new business or for one that's already established, the web is a gold mine of information, as well as an indispensable link to future customers, investors, and market opportunities.

What you'll learn from this chapter:

- How to research your market
- How to find business resources online
- How to find business plan consultants and competitions

# Information Grows Money

## Market Research

Thanks to the internet, market research for business planning purposes has become much easier and less time consuming. For example, by logging on to the U.S. Census Bureau website (www.census.gov), you can learn everything you need about population trends in your market, which helps you determine market share—a key piece of information in any business plan. Using your site or email, you can set up an online focus group to get a handle on what prospective customers want from a product or service like yours, how they'd use it, where they'd like to buy it, and how often they'd purchase it.

This kind of information will help you establish pricing, distribution, and promotional strategies.

You can garner a wealth of valuable information via the web on your competitors—and on businesses similar to yours operating in other markets. Visit these companies' websites to see what their product/service lines are, what their unique selling propositions are, who their target markets are and what media are used to reach them, what their prices are, and where and how their product is distributed. If their websites have a section called "News" or "Upcoming Events," you can learn about their plans for future marketing efforts and determine how they'll affect your business.

## Trade Associations: Key Source of Targeted Information

Trade associations are an excellent source of specific trade and industry information. Suppose you are an artisan specializing in concrete countertops and related items. Is there a trade association? Sure, see www.concretenetwork.com/newsletter.htm for specialized information.

Because there are more than 22,000 trade associations in the United States, you will be hard-pressed not to find one that will include your business. Most have periodicals—magazines or newsletters—whose editors are eager to justify their positions by providing the membership with up-to-date information of all kinds. You can call the editor directly (they like to hear from members) or send him an email with your particular questions.

Trade associations often sponsor trade shows, which can help you get information on suppliers, industry trends, consultants, and even seminars directly related to your business. The people you meet and the informal exchange of knowledge that results provide the greatest value: production tips, problem solutions, contacts, and ideas.

"By reading publications and reports available online, you can stay current with what's happening in your industry as well as plan for your business's future. You can look for industry classification codes on the North American Industry Classification System (NAICS) website. Once you find your

> industry code, you can use it in your search terms to find industry publications and articles."

## Communication

If your business is already established, use your website and social media presence to solicit valuable feedback from your customers. Stay in touch with them to foster customer loyalty. After a sale is made, ask them whether they're satisfied or if more service is needed. Let them know about upcoming events and specials. Ask them what changes, if any, they'd like to see made in your product or service and how it's delivered.

Keep in mind the 80-20 principle in business, which says that 80 percent of your business comes from repeat customers and 20 percent from new customers. Too many businesses spend an inordinate amount of money trying to lure new customers when their repeat customers and the friends, neighbors, colleagues, and family members of those regular customers are the backbone of most successful businesses.

Use the web and email to get the information you need about vendors and suppliers. Get a list of customers you can email, text, or phone so you can assess their business relationships before you make any commitments.

If you don't yet have your business up and running, you may want to tap into social media on your own to discuss your upcoming business— don't give too many secrets away, but go to online groups, discussions, or Facebook pages where you may find your demographic audience and start a conversation. See what they think in general about your ideas—get feedback.

## Financing Option

If your business plan will double as a financing proposal, visit the U.S. government's Small Business Administration site at www.sba.gov to learn more about the many different types of financing programs available. In addition to financial assistance through guaranteed loans, the SBA also offers counseling services, help in getting government contracts, management assistance through programs like SCORE (Service Corps of Retired Executives), and lots of publications.

Other government organizations also offer financing to small businesses, including the U.S. Department of Agriculture (www.rurdev.usda.gov) and the U.S. Department of Commerce's Export Assistance Centers (www.sba. gov/local-assistance/export-trade-assistance/us-export-assistance-centers). To find nongovernment organizations that provide financing to small businesses in your area, visit the Association for Enterprise Opportunity (AEO) at www.microenterpriseworks.org, and ask which programs serve businesses in your area. Your banker and state economic development office can also help.

>>> **plan of action**

Small Business Development Centers are one-stop shops set up by the Small Business Administration to give entrepreneurs free to low-cost advice, training, and technical assistance. There are SBDCs in each state and territory. Learn more online at www.sba.gov or call (800) 8-ASK-SBA.

## Books and How-To Manuals

Scores of books have been written on how to write a business plan. Most provide skimpy treatment of the issues while devoting many pages to sample plans. Sample plans are useful, but unless planners understand the principles of the planning process, they can't really create sophisticated, one-of-a-kind plans. The following books will help you with the details of various sections in your plan:

> *Dictionary of Business and Economics Terms* (Barron's). In its fifth edition, this compact, 800-page dictionary is a cure for jargon overexposure. It provides concise definitions of business and has appendices that explain common business acronyms, provide tables of compounded interest rate factors, and more. It's the kind of book you'll turn to again and again.

⟫ *Guerrilla Marketing in 30 Days, 3rd. ed.* (Entrepreneur Press), by Jay Conrad Levinson and Al Lautenslager. The most recent edition of this marketing classic provides updated marketing techniques for those with little cash but high hopes. Levinson's insistence on the central role of planning and his simple but effective explanations of how to do it will serve business planners well.

⟫ *What Every Angel Investor Wants You to Know: An Insider Reveals How to Get Smart Funding for Your Billion Dollar Idea* (McGraw Hill), by Brian Cohen and John Kador. If you want an inside and honest look at what angel investors think, this is a good book to get the perspective from the other side of the table. Cohen is chairman of the New York Angels, an independent consortium of individual accredited angel investors.

## Websites

The internet provides a virtually inexhaustible source of information for and about small business, including numerous sites with substantial databases of tips and ideas concerning business planning. Some of the best include the following:

⟫ *Entrepreneur.com.* This is the website of Entrepreneur Media, the nation's premier source for information for the entrepreneur and small business community and the parent corporation of this book's publisher. The site contains a vast array of information resources, practical advice, interviews with experts, profiles of successful entrepreneurs, product and service reviews, and more.

The site offers resources for new entrepreneurs, including sample business plans and sections on startups, marketing, and technology, all of which can be helpful while in your planning process.

The Entrepreneur website also hosts Entrepreneur Media's Bookstore (www.entrepreneur.com/bookstore), a source for books—including this one—that offer expert advice on starting, running, and growing a small business. These include business startup guides, step-by-step startup guides to specific businesses, and business management guides, which offer in-depth information on financing, marketing, and more.

*Small Business Administration (www.sba.gov).* The SBA's website is a vast directory to services provided by the federal agency devoted to helping small businesses. These include special lending programs, electronic databases of minority- and disadvantaged-owned businesses, directories of government contracting opportunities, and more.

There is also a generous selection of answers to frequently asked questions, tip sheets, and other advice. You can get a list of questions to ask yourself to see if you have the personality of an entrepreneur, find help with selecting a business, and browse an entire area devoted to help with your business plan.

BPlans.com. Bplans offers a very comprehensive website with a host of information about all aspects of business plans, as well as starting and growing a business. Funding, tools for creating a plan, and robust business plan guides and templates are all available at bplans.com/business-planning/.

## Trade Groups and Associations

You're not in this alone. There are countless local and national organizations, both public and private, devoted to helping small businesses get up and running. They provide services ranging from low-rent facilities to financial assistance, from help in obtaining government contracts to help with basic business planning issues. Many of these services are provided for free or at nominal cost.

▷ *SCORE.* The Service Corps of Retired Executives, known as SCORE, is a nonprofit group of mostly retired businesspeople who volunteer to provide counseling to small businesses at no charge. SCORE has been around since 1964 and has helped more than three million entrepreneurs and aspiring entrepreneurs. SCORE is a source for all kinds of business advice, from how to write a business plan to investigating marketing potential and managing cash flow.

▷ SCORE counselors work out of nearly 400 local chapters throughout the United States. You can obtain a referral to a counselor in your local chapter by contacting the national office. For more information, visit Score.org or call (800) 634-0245.

▷ *International Business Innovation Association.* The InBIA is the global organization for business incubators, which are organizations specially set up to nurture young firms and help them survive and grow. Incubators provide leased office facilities on flexible terms, shared business services, management assistance, help in obtaining financing, and technical support. For more information, visit inbia. org or call it at (407) 965-5653.

▷ *Chambers of Commerce.* The many chambers of commerce throughout the United States are organizations devoted to providing networking, lobbying, training, and more. If you think chambers are all about having lunch with a bunch of community boosters, think again. Among the services the U.S. Chamber of Commerce offers is a web-based business solutions program that provides online help with specific small business needs, including planning, marketing, and other tasks such as creating a press release, collecting a bad debt, recruiting employees, and creating a retirement plan.

The U.S. Chamber of Commerce is the umbrella organization for local chambers, of which there are more than 1,000 in the United States. If you're planning on doing business overseas, don't forget to check for an American chamber of commerce in the countries where you hope to have a presence. They are set up to provide information and assistance to U.S. firms seeking to do business there. Many, but not all, countries have American chambers. You can find the national chamber of commerce at USChamber.com or call its Washington headquarters at (800) 638-6582.

## Hire Power

If you decide to hire a consultant to help you prepare your plan, take care that you select the right person. Here are the guidelines:

- *Get referrals.* Ask colleagues, acquaintances, and professionals such as bankers, accountants, and lawyers for the names of business plan consultants they recommend. A good referral goes a long way to easing concerns you may have. Few consultants advertise anyway, so referrals may be your only choice.
- *Look for a fit.* Find a consultant who is an expert in helping businesses like yours. Ideally, the consultant should have lots of experience with companies of similar size and age in similar industries. Avoid general business experts or those who lack experience in your field.
- *Check references.* Get the names of at least three clients the consultant has helped to write plans. Call the former clients and ask about the consultant's performance. Was the consultant's final fee in line with the original estimate? Was the plan completed on time? Did it serve the intended purpose?
- *Get it in writing.* Have a legal contract for the consultant's services. It should discuss in detail the fee, when it will be paid, and under what circumstances. And make sure you get a detailed, written description of what the consultant must do to earn the fee. Whether it's an hourly rate or a flat fee isn't as important as each party knowing exactly what's expected.

## Business Plan Consultants

Businesspeople tend to fall into two camps when it comes to consultants. Some believe strongly in the utility and value of hiring outside experts to bring new perspective and broad knowledge to challenging tasks. Others feel consultants are overpaid yes-men brought in only to endorse plans already decided upon or to take the heat for unpopular but necessary decisions.

Who's right? Both are, depending on the consultant you hire and your purpose for hiring one. Most consultants are legitimate experts in specific or general business areas. And most consultants can be hired to help with all or part of the process of writing a business plan.

The downside is you have to spend a lot of time on communication before and during the process of working with a consultant. Be sure you have fully explained, and the consultant fully understands, the nature of your business, your concept and strategy, your financial needs, and other matters such as control, future plans, and so on. Refer to these important issues throughout the process—you don't want to pay for a beautifully done plan that fits somebody else's business, not yours. And when the work is done, debrief the consultant to find out if there's anything you can learn that wasn't included in the plan.

### The Lowdown on Consultants

A good consultant should provide the following:

1. *She should lay out expectations.* In any working relationship, you need to know exactly what is expected of whom you are hiring.
2. *The consultant should only make promises she can keep.* Hold her to her word. Business is about making and keeping promises.
3. *All plans should be made in advance and make promises that were inherently discussed beforehand.* Without a concrete plan a consultant can "wing it," leaving you

without any way to look at milestones and keep tabs on her progress.

4. *A consultant should provide regular, specific updates.* You need to set up a schedule and a means of regular communication. You want to know—specifically— what she is doing, and this means regular ongoing communication, which is an integral part of a healthy business relationship.

5. *She should not have a personal agenda.* If the consultant is not acting in the best interest of your company, then she is not doing the job ethically. Make sure anyone you're hiring is working for your needs, not theirs.

## Business Plan Competitions

If you happen to be a business student, you may be able to enter your business plan in a college business plan competition. These competitions, of which there are more than three dozen in the United States, confer a measure of fame and even some money on the winners. A panel of plan experts including college professors, venture capitalists, and bankers usually judge entries.

Winners are the plans that best lay out a convincing case for a business's success. Judges can be tough; contestants can expect scathing criticism of poorly thought-out plans.

Venture Labs Investment Competition is the name of the best known of the nation's business plan competitions. It's sponsored by the University of Texas at Austin. Venture Labs Investment Competition calls itself the "Super Bowl of world business-plan competition" and is the oldest of the approximately three dozen business school-sponsored plan competitions. More than two dozen plan-writing teams from as far away as Australia participate in the contest, which began in 1983.

Another major competition is the Rice Business Plan Competition. This very prestigious three-day competition is the largest and richest graduate-level student startup competition with more than $1 million in cash and prizes. More information is at https://rbpc.rice.edu/.

You'll also find competitions that are not sponsored by universities or business schools such as New York Start Up, an annual competition for New Yorkers starting for-profit businesses that offers cash prizes totaling up to $15,000. Sponsored by the New York Public Library and Wells Fargo, the competition began in 2010. For more, go to https://sites.google.com/nypl.org/nystartupbizplancomp-/home.

There are numerous state competitions such as the Rhode Island Business Competition. Started in 2000 by Garrett Hunter, then president of the Business Development Company of Rhode Island, the annual competition is designed for new businesses as well as those in the early development stages. Prizes of cash and in-kind services with a total value of at least $150,000 are awarded to a winner and two finalists. You can learn more at https://ri-business.com/.

### Hackathons

Also known as hack days, a hack weekend, or a hackfest, a hackathon is an event (usually lasting a weekend) in which programmers, software developers, interface designers, and others team up to create software, apps, or some useful technology. Typically, the process emerges from brainstorming sessions to explore and discuss ideas. Then they move to implementing the best ones. In the end there are hackathon winners in competitions such as HackMIT, presented by the university, or hackNY, co-organized by NYU and Columbia University.

In a slight variation of the hackathon, the hackaplan has emerged. In short, the goal of a hackaplan is the same as a hackathon, but with diverse business teams as opposed to programmers. The objective is for each team to create a business plan rather than software or an app. While there may certainly be a lot of tweaking of the final product, a weekend of brainstorming on a business plan can jump-start the process.

## What Does It All Mean?

In the end, consultants can only help you know what it is you're looking to accomplish with your business. Business plan competitions can give you a leg up on the competition, but you will then need to use that edge wisely by putting your award-winning plan into the right hands. SCORE and other organizations can benefit you in the business planning process, if you are ready to listen, learn, and ask questions.

Remember, though, there is no magic formula for success. Your business plan should lay down the foundation from which you will do everything you can to build and sustain a successful business. It should tell the story of your business going forward and help you think hard about every aspect of your business. It should help you make the key decisions as you proceed. It should also keep you thinking about all of the possibilities.

Writing a business plan is not easy, but neither is starting and running a successful business. Many new businesses (as well as older ones) fail every year. Some have no concrete plan, others have drifted from the plan, and many have lost the motivation to grow and change to keep pace with the changing marketplace. Complacency stops many businesses from taking the next steps.

A business plan means what you want it to mean. It can be a way of guiding you through the process, a means of getting investors, a way of finding advisors, a document to help lure new talent, or all of the above. It is not something that you finish and forget to look at, but instead something you can go back to, just as you would do with a blueprint of a house or a building as you plan to add on a new room or rewire the facility.

### Elevator Pitch

Sometimes there is simply not enough time for someone to read your business plan or even hear a full presentation. Therefore, you need an elevator pitch. It is the ultra-short version of your plan featuring only the most significant of significant information, all presented in the time it takes for an elevator ride. Of course, the elevator pitch cannot replace the well-though-out, detailed business plan, but it can drum up interest in reading one. Have such a pitch written, rehearsed, and ready to go. And, keep in mind, it can be harder to write the twenty- to thirty-second elevator pitch than the entire business plan. Each and every word carries more weight because (like on Twitter) you are very limited.

If you want to see winning elevator pitches by other business owners, check out the Entrepreneur Elevator Pitch show online at https://www.entrepreneur.com/video/series/elevatorpitch. It's in its eighth season as of this writing, and watching these videos will give you the tips you need to craft your own elevator pitch that will win you the deal!

Of course, the business plan is worthwhile only if you are honest in what you put on paper, meaning being honest to yourself. If you are writing down an idealized version of what you'd like to see without including well-researched facts and forecasts that are based on due diligence, then your business plan will simply lead you to disappointment. Therefore, as you write the plan, stop and look at it periodically to make sure you are being realistic and have other people you know and trust read it to confirm that you are being forthright and not overly optimistic.

The real optimism of a business plan is creating something that you can accomplish and make successful over time. It's fine to use the business plan to shoot for the stars—but start with one star at a time.

# LivePlan

## Get the #1 Rated Business Plan Software - Free

Easily write your business plan, impress investors, and gain the insights you need to grow!

Your purchase of Write Your Business Plan includes one month of free access to LivePlan Premium. As part of this exclusive bundle, simply use your mobile device to scan the code below, or follow the link, and get your first month of LivePlan free of charge.

Or visit liveplan.com/emibook

**What are you waiting for? Start your business plan today.**

# About the Author

Eric Butow is the owner of Butow Communications Group (BCG) in Jackson, California (butow.net). BCG offers website development, online marketing, and writing services. He has written or cowritten over forty books, most recently Grow Your Business (Entrepreneur Press), Instagram for Business for Dummies, Second Edition (Wiley), MCA Microsoft Office Specialist (Office 365 and Office 2019) Complete Study Guide (Sybex), Digital Etiquette for Dummies (Wiley), and Instagram for Dummies, Second Edition (Wiley). Eric has also developed and taught networking, computing, and usability courses for Ed2Go; Virtual Training Company; California State University, Sacramento; and Udemy.

When he's not working in (and on) his business or writing books, you can find Eric enjoying time with friends, walking around the historic Gold Rush town of Jackson, and helping his mother manage her infant and toddler day-care business.

# About the Contributors

*Tim Berry | Founder and Chairman Palo Alto Software*

Palo Alto Software founder Tim Berry pioneered business plan software, is a recognized expert in business planning, and quite literally wrote the book on Lean Planning. He has a Stanford MBA and degrees with honors from the University of Oregon and the University of Notre Dame. He taught "Starting a Business" at the University of Oregon for eleven years and is a blogger and speaker on the topic of business planning. He's the expert other experts turn to; he's been interviewed on business planning by CNN, Forbes, USA Today, Guy Kawasaki, and others. Small business radio host Jim Blasingame calls him "the world guru on business planning."

## Sabrina Parsons | CEO Palo Alto Software

Sabrina has served as CEO of Palo Alto Software since 2007, and has overseen the company's transformative transition from a desktop software company to a cloud-based software company. A graduate of Princeton University, she previously held leadership positions at Commtouch and Epinions, and founded her own web consulting company. As a passionate leader in and supporter of her local community, Sabrina contributes her time and expertise as a board member and technology advisor of a multitude of non-profit organizations, such as the Princeton Entrepreneurs Network, Oregon Community Foundation, Eugene Area Chamber of Commerce, and a number of community organizations in Eugene. She participates as a judge for business plan competitions across the U.S., and speaks on business planning, leadership, and women in technology.

## Noah Parsons | COO Palo Alto Software

Before joining Palo Alto Software, Noah was an early internet marketing expert in the Silicon Valley. He joined Yahoo! in 1996 as one of its first 101 employees and became producer of the Yahoo! Employment property as part of the Yahoo! Classifieds team, before leaving to serve as director of production at Epinions.com. He is a graduate of Princeton University. Noah devotes most of his free time to his three sons. In the winter you'll find him giving them lessons on the ski slopes, and in summer they're usually involved in a variety of outdoor pursuits.

## Trevor Betenson | CFO Palo Alto Software

Trevor is responsible for leading the company's accounting and finance efforts. He has spent time working as a financial controller in ad agencies, as well as in the healthcare and transportation industries. Before joining Palo Alto Software, Trevor was the assistant controller for publicly traded McCann Erickson at their Salt Lake City, UT office. Trevor is a School of Accountancy graduate from Utah State University, and earned his MBA from the Jon M. Huntsman School of Business at Utah State University. An avid track and field fan, Trevor also enjoys hiking and camping with his wife and three daughters.

# Appendices

# Business and Business Plan Resources

## Websites

Angelcapitalassociation.org—For locating angel investors

Bizfilings.com—Information for small business owners

Bizplan.com

Bloomberg.com/businessweek

Bplans.com

CNN.com/business

Economist.com

Entrepreneur.com

Forbes.com

FundingPost.com—Events that include angel investors and VCs

Gust.com—Angel investor networks

Inc.com/business-plans

Nolo.com—Legal forms and information

Nvca.org—National Venture Capitalist Association

SBA.gov—Small Business Association

Score.org—Volunteer mentors and advisors; they also have business
plan templates at: Score.org/resources/business-plan-template-
startup-business

## Books

*Anatomy of a Business Plan: The Step-by-Step Guide to Building a
Business and Securing Your Company's Future* by Linda Pinson, 8th
edition, Out Of Your Mind and into the Market, 2013

*Cash from the Crowd* by Sally Outlaw, Entrepreneur Press, 2013 (ebook)

*How to Write a Business Plan* by Mike McKeever, 14th edition,
NOLO, 2018

*Legal Forms for Starting & Running a Small Business* by Fred S. Steingold,
12th edition, NOLO, 2022

*The Marketing Plan Handbook* by Robert Bly, 2nd Edition, Entrepreneur
Press, 2015

*Networking Like a Pro* by Ivan Misner, Ph.D., 2nd Edition, Entrepreneur
Press, 2017

*Start Your Own Business: The Only Startup Book You'll Ever Need* by
the Staff of Entrepreneur Media, Inc., 8th edition, Entrepreneur
Press, 2021

*Start Your Own e-Business* by Entrepreneur Press and Rich Mintzer, 3rd
Edition, Entrepreneur Press, 2014

*Successful Business Plan: Secrets & Strategies* by Rhonda Abrams, 7th
edition, Planning Shop, 2019

*Your First Business Plan* by Joseph A. Covello and Brian Hazelgren,
Sourcebooks, 2005

*FYI:* All books from Entrepreneur Press can be found at Entrepreneur.
com/bookstore.

## Online Business Plan Courses

The Right-Brain Business Plan® Home Study e-Course:
www.rightbrainbusinessplan.com/courses

SBA Small Business Learning Center—How to Write a Business Plan:
learn.sba.gov/learning-center-plan/learning-center-how-to-write-a-
business-plan

Udemy.com—Create a Damn Good Business Plan:
www.udemy.com/create-a-damn-good-business-plan

Universal Class—How to Write a Business Plan 101:
www.universalclass.com/i/course/how-to-write-a-business-plan.htm

# Glossary

**balloon payment**—A single, usually final, payment on a loan that is much greater than the payments preceding it; some business loans, for example, require interest-only payments the first year or two, followed by a single large payment that repays all the principal.

**branding**—The marketing practice of creating a name, symbol, or design that identifies and differentiates a product from other products; well-known brands include Tide, Dockers, and Dell.

**business concept**—The basic idea around which a business is built. For instance, FedEx is built on the idea of overnight delivery, while Amazon.com was originally built around the idea of selling books over the internet.

**cash conversion cycle**—The amount of time it takes to transform your cash outlays into cash income; for a manufacturer, the number of days or weeks required to purchase raw materials and turn them into inventory, then sales, and, finally, collections.

**competitive advantage**—Factor or factors that give a business an advantage over its competitors. This can be based on the quality of products or services, lower prices, better customer service, faster delivery, and/or all of the above.

**co-op promotion**—Arrangement between two or more businesses to cross-promote their enterprises to customers.

**current assets**—Assets likely to be turned into cash within a year.

**current liabilities**—Amounts you owe and are to pay in less than a year, such as accounts payable to suppliers and short-term loans.

**due diligence**—Doing research to find data on a business, company, customers, lender, vendor, or any individual or group with whom you may potentially do business.

**EBIT**—An accounting term for a company's operational earnings separate from the effects of interest payments and taxation.

**e-commerce or electronic commerce**—Selling products and services through sites on the internet.

**executive summary**—Section of a business plan that briefly describes what the rest of the plan contains; also the first section of the plan, often written after the other sections.

**factoring**—The flip side of trade credit; what happens when a supplier sells its accounts receivables to a financial specialist called a factor. The factor immediately pays the amount of the receivables, less a discount, and receives the payments when they arrive from customers; an important form of finance in many industries.

**forecast**—To forecast is to use prior data to determine upcoming trends. Forecasting can prove very helpful for budgeting and marketing purposes. In a business plan for a startup, forecasting can indicate that you have utilized historical data within your industry to predict future results.

**initial public offering (IPO)**—The first sale of stock by a private company to the public. Typically IPOs are issued by smaller, younger companies seeking capital to expand. However, established companies can issue one later on to generate additional funding.

**limited liability corporation**—Business legal structure resembling an S corporation but allowing owners more flexibility in dividing up profits while still providing protection from liability; abbreviated LLC.

**liquidity**—A company's ability to convert noncash assets, such as inventory and accounts receivable, into cash; essentially, the company's ability to pay its bills.

**logistics**—The science of moving objects, such as product inventory, from one location to another.

**management team**—The key personnel that have significant roles in managing and running the business. They need to be profiled in the management section of a business plan.

**marketing plan**—Part of your business plan, and something that you will update regularly. Such a plan outlines how you will spread the word about your product and/or services. It includes everything from advertising to promotional messages to web presence to giveaway items with your company name or logo.

**mission statement**—A sentence or two describing a company's function, markets, and competitive advantages.

**objectives**—Long-term aims, frequently representing the ultimate level to which you aspire.

**organization, functional**—A company or other entity with a structure that divides authority along functions such as marketing, finance, and so on; these functions cross product lines and other boundaries.

**organization, line**—A company or other entity with a structure divided by product lines, means of production, industries served, and so on; each line may have its own support staff for the various functions.

**organization, line and staff**—A company or other entity with a structure calling for staff managers, like planners and accountants, to act as advisors supporting a line manager, such as the operations vice president.

**outsourcing**—Having a component or service performed or supplied by an outside firm or individual; used to reduce time and money costs for support work and add flexibility in production staffing.

**positioning**—Marketing tool that describes a product or service in reference to its position in the marketplace; for example, the newest, smallest, cheapest, or second largest.

**rate of return**—The income or profit earned by an investor on capital invested into a company; usually expressed as an annual percentage.

**search engine optimization (SEO)**—Utilizing keywords and other strategies in order to position your website to come up higher during an online web search.

**target market**—The audience most likely to buy your goods or services, usually found as the result of demographic research

**turnaround**—A reversal in a company's fortunes, taking it from near death to robust health or the revival of a failing company to more profitable status.

**unique selling proposition**—The factor or consideration presented by a seller as the reason that one product or service is different from, and better than, the competition.

**vision statement**—A sentence or two describing a company's long-range aims, such as achieving a dominant market share or attaining a reputation for world-class quality.

**working capital**—The amount of money a business has in cash, accounts receivable, inventory, and other current assets; normally refers to net working capital, which is current assets minus current liabilities.

# Index